His Brunette Alibi

Book Three of the Homeless Man's Killer Series

Karen Roberts

His Brunette Alibi

The contents of this work are true. This book is written witness testimony to assist authorities in the United States and Canada in the criminal prosecution of Daniel James Bondehagen. The author and publisher assumes all responsibility and liability for the publication of this work.

All Rights Reserved
Copyright © 2024 by KK Roberts Books

Library of Congress Registration Number TXu 2-458-949
Printed in the United States of America, 2025
Cover design by: Diego Sanguino

No part of this book may be reproduced or transmitted, downloaded, distributed, emailed, reverse engineered, converted to pdf format, or stored in or introduced into any information storage and retrieval system, in any form or by any means, including photocopying or recording, whether electronic or mechanical, now known or hereinafter invented without permission in writing from KK Roberts Books.

KK Roberts Books
PO Box 363
Ridgefield, WA 98642
website at KKRobertsBooks.com

Hardback ISBN: 979-8-9912353-3-4
Paperback ISBN: 979-8-9912353-4-1
EBook: Kindle Edition 979-8-9886431-9-7

Table of Contents

How Do You Know It Was Six Hours?
Sol Duc Falls, Olympic Mountains – June 17, 1984
Bathtub for Turtles – June 18, 1984
Orcas Island – June 19, 1984
Vancouver, British Columbia – June 20, 1984
When Did I Smell That? - Meet Me at the Pier
Returning to the Hotel - Vancouver, B.C. June 20, 1984
British Columbia, Canada – June 21, 1984
Holes in the Wall– My Childhood, April 1983
Japanese Art - Daniel's Childhood 1968
Daniel's Adolescence - 1978
Returning to My Apartment- November 1983
Character Play – Summer 1984
One last attempt at camping - late Summer 1984
North Queen Anne - February 1984
Beaten to Light Purple – September 1984
In the One Bedroom
The Fox Trot
Headboard
S & M
Empowerment
On the Other Side of McDonalds
Stirred Light Green
Filling in the Dark Space
Lying Dog
Hardness of Hearts
Cutting In
Death of the Killer Clown - May 10, 1994
Camping Gear

Moving On
Stalker Returns
The New Nature Trail
George Floyd - May 25, 2020
Tempered Glass - Downtown Seattle 1985
Riot Broke Out - Downtown Portland 2020
Another Nature Walk
Sub USB
Diary Entries
Conclusion

How Do You Know It Was Six Hours?

Before Daniel James Bondehagen was captured by the U.S. Marshal, I was contacted by an agent from the Federal Bureau of Investigation. These calls weren't alarming. On the contrary, they were breaks of sanity in the icy crust of a world that facilitated Daniel's domination of my reality. This psychological abuse was worse since a 1986 protection order prevented his domination in the bedroom. It seemed from Daniel's perspective, distorting actual events and painting me as forgetful were sadistic aphrodisiacs.

"You said he was gone from the tent for six hours," the FBI agent noted in the phone call.

"Yes," I answered. "My husband was gone for six hours that night." We had two nights of camping on our honeymoon.

I married Daniel Bondehagen at eighteen, forty years ago, in 1984. Daniel was a tall, thin Norwegian man with blonde hair and blue eyes, who looked similar to Tom Petty. "I don't need to grow my hair long, because I know exactly what that would look like," Daniel said.

Daniel aspired to become a minister. He was motivated by the youth pastor who provided his counseling. But his career goal was far from a possibility. We divorced in King County on March 17, 1987.

In 2024, the number of his murder convictions changes each time I look. News coverage is limited while the court hearings are conducted. At my last check, Bondehagen has 26 murder convictions, one more than Ted Bundy, and the authorities haven't finished prosecuting the murder charges.

[In the United States the murder convictions ended at 185. Daniel Bondehagen was transported to Canada for murder trials there. So far, he has confessed to the murders, hoping to be a household name like Ted Bundy. More murders in the U.S. remain incomplete. Despite all the times I've been proven correct, I couldn't get the authorities in the United States to trust my reports. It is very disappointing for the psychological abuse to continue while Bondehagen is in prison. By now I thought I would be free from the assumption that I made a false complaint. Very truly, I have never made a false complaint.]

In *The Whiffle Ball Killer*, I wrote about Daniel Bondehagen's first murder and human trafficking. *Profile in the Shadows* was about the cons and hoaxes he played and the murders of those he knew. Last, but certainly not least, are the murders that seemed to be random. But nothing Daniel Bondehagen did was truly random. There was always a plan behind it. As I write this account, I often find that he used me as his brunette alibi.

"How do you know it was six hours?" the FBI agent continued.

"I looked at my watch," I replied.

"When he came back?" the FBI agent asked, "Or when he left?"

"Both," I answered. That seemed obvious. I recorded two numbers to subtract and calculate the length of time.

"What made you think of looking at your watch the first time," the FBI agent asked.

"Oh," I gasped, "I hadn't thought about it. Daniel was already irritating me with his absences." The agent had a smart question. Punctuality was emphasized in my family. If someone was late, we knew exactly how many minutes they were tardy.

"When?" the FBI agent asked.

"When he was spying on me at Orcas Island, while I was at a tourist viewpoint," I answered. On Orcas Island, I stepped out of the passenger seat to look over the water. We had changed drivers after the ferry and would change back after this stop. The sky was light blue with white clouds. The impressive rocks were tall and brownish gray. The wind was cool, and slightly uncomfortable despite the summer day. The water was blue with small waves and would have been inviting if the distance below was not so steep. I turned to my left to share the beautiful view with Daniel, only to find him missing. He was missing for a long time. I sat on the rock edge and sulked.

Two young men approached me and said, "There is something wrong with that guy."

I turned to look at them. They might have been college students. Daniel stepped out into the open. He was watching from a distance to my right. He took my picture, as I became more frustrated trying to find him. I hadn't expected he would just watch me. I realized he had already practiced stalking me at the grocery store. This was at the Piggly Wiggly in Auburn. He said it was a fun place to shop. And then I spent ninety minutes trying to find him. He was hiding behind the store shelves, gloating over my frustration.

"We will give you a ride home," the young men offered. "You don't need to bother with him."

"No," I answered. "It's okay. He is my husband. This is our honeymoon. And it is my car that we are driving. In fact, it is my turn to drive."

That was not the answer they were expecting. One of the young men glanced over his left shoulder towards my car, "You could leave him behind." He was serious.

I chuckled. That might be nice on one level, but I did not believe turnabout was fair play. Daniel emerged from behind his viewpoint and was ready to travel again. In his practical joke, scenic viewpoint meant viewing me as I became frustrated. That was all I could remember at the time the FBI agent asked. But there were more absences, many more, too many.

Daniel's version of the events of our honeymoon week is very different from mine. I'm looking deeper into that week and evaluating all of his absences. Dates are included to assist the authorities in his prosecution. Some events I mentioned previously in the series are included again, as I fill in the dark spaces of time in between.

Sol Duc Falls, Olympic Mountains – June 1984

Daniel said he loved camping. It was something we had in common. He said he preferred hike-in camping, in a secluded spot, breaking camp to move on at the crack of dawn, and leaving no litter behind. He wanted to be near a clear lake or river to bathe in.

I was thinking about skinny dipping together on our honeymoon, out in nature, the trees creating seclusion, away from other things in life, only the birds to view us. And this plan suited me fine. In my mind, I thought this would be an opportunity to enjoy each other.

Daniel had other plans. On June 17, 1984, we drove to Clallam County and parked my 1972 Chevrolet Nova at the Sol Duc campgrounds parking lot. I was tasked with packing all of the camping supplies before the trip. This was one extra thing thrown on my plate along with planning the wedding and honeymoon. I didn't pack my backpack. I hadn't expected to. The backpack was intended for my college books, not for camping. Daniel was upset at me for forgetting my backpack and required me to carry a thermos he purchased at a garage sale.

We walked one mile down Lover's Lane Trail along Soleduck River. I expected this would be romantic, but he rolled his eyes and wouldn't hold my hand. He thought I was being childish. My arms began to feel heavy from carrying the thermos. The thermos had a cork. I pulled out the cork to take a swig of the water. I took a drink from the thermos and felt a fizz in my mouth. It tasted like home-canned apple sauce gone bad with botulism. I spit it out in a fast spray and added more spit to clean out my mouth. I felt bad for Daniel that his important thermos held undrinkable fluid.

We hiked until the trail crossed over Soleduck River twice, and then bent to be right along the river. There we found a spot to pitch our tent. The sky was blue, and the sun peaked through the tree leaves. The forest air was cool but comfortable. We could hear the water rushing over the rocks. It was clear and drinkable snow melt. I took the thermos to the river and poured out the contents. A clear gelatinous substance reluctantly made its way out of the thermos. I used the river current to fully rinse the thermos out and replaced it with fresh clean water. I brought the thermos to Daniel, but he refused to take a drink. I sat down and drank the river water.

Daniel opened a can of Coke, drank it, and opted not to start a fire. A woman and her daughter hiked past our tent to the east. They both had long, straight brown hair, brown eyes, and fair skin. They greeted us with warm smiles and a hand wave as they walked past.

After some time had passed, "I didn't see them come back through," Daniel commented.

"I didn't either," I answered. I sat and enjoyed nature, the delicate splashing of the river over the rocks.

"Where do you think they were going?" Daniel asked.

I got out my Olympic Mountains trail map to check. "The Lover's Lane Trail continued on to the east to intersect with Deer Lake Trail, just before the Sol Duc Falls viewpoint," I said. "The campground was at the beginning of the trail to the west."

"Oh, that's right," Daniel said, "the campsite," looking to the west.

Daniel hiked on to see where they camped. He came back and reported, "I found where they are camping." Their campsite was near Deer Lake Trail. "There are men there," Daniel said.

I offered to cook dinner over a fire or camp stove, but Daniel said, "No." We ate cold food and drank the river water before going to bed. "Any colder and it would be like ice," Daniel commented.

"That's fresh snow melt," I praised. Good clean water for drinking or anything needed.

The mountain air made the night chilly. Daniel didn't want to zip our sleeping bags together. He was warm and comfortable in his own sleeping bag, wearing his long thermal underwear. He left our tent at about three in the morning. I didn't check my watch, because it was too dark, and I hadn't gotten into that habit yet. When he came back, he said, "I needed to use the bathroom." And that was the reason he was gone. He said, "There was a mother deer and her fawn outside our tent."

I went outside to see. The mother deer and her fawn were not frightened of me at all and let me take pictures of them from behind a mossy-sided tree. I smiled to realize that I could tell which direction was north. I felt at the moss for reassurance. It was peaceful and calm, the air was fresh with positive oxygen, and the green leaves on the trees provided a pleasant cover. The sun was coming up and glistening brightly on the water of Soleduck River. It was now June 18, 1984.

When I returned to the tent, I found Daniel had just taken it down. "I already took a bath in the river," he said, tightly rolling up a blanket to place into his backpack. He must have taken a bath in the river in the early morning before coming back to the tent.

I had hoped we could bathe in the river together, as a romantic moment. Now that wasn't possible. And worse, as I looked around, I had no place to change out of my pajamas. "I can't hike back like this," I complained. I expected to heat water over the camp stove to clean up. "At least let me boil some water."

"No time," Daniel responded, impatiently looking over his shoulder toward Sol Duc Falls.

"I need to change into my jeans, at least," I complained. I didn't want to walk back down "Lover's Lane" in my pajama bottoms.

"Just change out in the open," Daniel decided. He was losing his patience. He shook his head at me. "You didn't need to spend so much time taking pictures of the deer."

I gasped. I thought he would appreciate that I captured the beautiful memories of our honeymoon together. I changed out of my pajamas, looking over my shoulder. I mainly looked towards the campground worried about early morning hikers, but then remembered I also needed to be concerned about someone hiking back towards the campground. Although it was too early in the morning for that. And Daniel seemed to have that direction covered. No one came through. We left to hike back. The idea of camping to enjoy nature was not in his thoughts.

This time Daniel, carried the thermos with the camping gear. I asked, "Why couldn't you carry the thermos on the way in?"

"I wanted to punish you for not packing the correct gear," Daniel snapped.

I wondered. Why did he act this way? Was he reliving his father's World War II experience or at war in his head?

When we reached the Sol Duc camping area, he wanted to go straight out and not stop at the restrooms. I accommodated him and went straight to the driver's seat.

On the way out, instead of turning right onto Highway 101, he wanted me to take a left. "It will be more scenic," Daniel promised. He had me turn onto Highway 113 and then double back by turning onto Highway 112. This added an extra hour to the trip. The road was very windy, exhausting, and ugly. Mud-covered tree stumps protruded out of a smelly swamp. Tree branches held back the sun from our view. The other route would have taken us next to the beautiful blue water, with the sunrise glistening off the surface.

I needed to use the restroom. Daniel kept telling me to wait. When we reached Highway 101, this time going in the right direction, he looked behind us and cheered at his success, "We are back onto the main road! Look at that."

I shook my head in irritation. We finally stopped in Port Angeles and grabbed muffins for breakfast in a to-go bag. Daniel shook his head at sitting down in the cafe. I used the portable outhouse near the parking lot. Then we continued on to Anacortes.

Bathtub for Turtles

"Look at this bathtub," Daniel said, "It's for turtles." He laughed.

"Turtles?" I asked. I came to view the bathtub. It was confusing. I realized he was talking about the size of the tub.

"Should we find some turtles and put them in there?" Daniel asked with a chuckle.

"Well, I guess I won't be shaving my legs in this," I answered.

We slept in the same bed that night and finally broke the ice. It wasn't so much romantic, as it was about what goes where? It was awkward and uncomfortable, at first. Later we tried again, and everything came together more smoothly.

In the morning, "For the first time in my life, I feel satisfied," Daniel said as he lay flat on the bed. It was a startling comment, after making love for the first time as husband and wife. I wondered what he was comparing me to.

We left to get onto the ferry for the San Juan Islands. Daniel was gone for a moment and a man on the ferry approached me, "You need to have a talk with him," he said. "I caught him rewinding his camera and opening the back to expose the film."

I rolled my eyes. "That is my camera," I explained. "Maybe he doesn't know how to use it." The pictures of the deer were on that film and the main pictures that I cared about. I wondered how incompetent my new husband was. *I didn't think he was intentional and devious.* I explained to the other passenger, "We are on our honeymoon, and he seems to think the time together is for watching television." I referred to the first two nights of our honeymoon without sex.

The man on the ferry responded, "He needed to have some things explained to him by his parents." He was there with his wife and two sons, and he needed to return to his family.

I nodded and waved goodbye. For the first time, I was thankful that my parents were more proactive in explaining things. "You need to wait until the number at the top reads just past 24, see where it turns red, keep the back of the camera closed, and then rewind the film," I explained. "When this number goes back to the start, then you can open the back of the camera." I changed out the film and made a mental note not to let him use it again without my supervision.

Daniel dashed off. He was back at the car again when it was time to leave the ferry, sitting in the driver's seat. I sat down in the passenger seat. We stopped at the scenic viewpoint where Daniel hid from me, a situation I described to the FBI. Then we continued on the road.

Orcas Island

I took over driving on Orcas Island, Daniel wanted me to take a variety of backroads instead of the main road. "Turn here, now turn here, okay, now turn here."

These extra turns were wasting gas, and we didn't pass any gas stations on those less-traveled roads. "We need to stop and get gas!" I said in a panic. "This isn't funny."

We found a gas station with high prices. "That worked better than I thought," Daniel said. "No one will know when we arrived."

I didn't see how the diversion was an accomplishment. We could have had better gas prices on the more traveled roads. We checked into the hotel at Orcas Island. The room had two queen-sized beds. "We'll use both of them," Daniel said.

I envisioned making love in one bed, and then in the other. "Okay," I said, first hesitantly, and then on a second thought with more enthusiasm. I was ready for another night of twice. Why not?

Daniel settled down onto the first Queen bed, on the right, and used the remote to turn on the television. He found the Star Wars movie and played it loudly.

I laid down next to him on the Queen bed on his right side.

Daniel wanted to watch television and do nothing else. Daniel motioned for me to sleep in the other bed by looking at me, looking at the bed to the other side, and jerking his head towards the right.

I didn't move. This was confusing. I didn't know what his head jerk meant. Was he worried about the neighbors complaining about the sound of the television?

"Do you want me to carry you to the door?" Daniel asked in irritation.

I thought maybe he was referring to a ritual that we missed. "Can you lift me? Am I too heavy?" I asked. I envisioned him carrying me over the threshold. He had criticized the custom as one of inequality when we were engaged. Maybe he changed his mind?

Daniel came around to the other side of the bed and picked me up. He carried me over to the door, put me outside, went back into the hotel room, and locked the door behind him.

I was now locked out of my own hotel room. I decided to explore the grounds and landscaping. The grass was green and mowed. There weren't any flowers. There was a distant view of the water. I had to stand in the right place to see it. This wasn't what the brochure had shown.

Closer to the main office there was a swimming pool, but I didn't bring my swimsuit. A few guests were sitting around the pool in deep conversation. No one was in the water. I mentioned to the guests at the pool that I was locked out of my room. They pointed to the main office. I stepped into the main office, which was a small area with a desk and little boxes on the wall. I talked to the hotel receptionist and told him I was locked out.

The hotel receptionist, dressed in a black suit, locked up the main office to walk back to my room with me. I explained that I wouldn't complain, but I had reserved and paid for the room.

The resort had rented the room to me; I was entitled to entry. The hotel receptionist decided to treat the matter as someone else in my room.

He knocked twice on the door with master room keys in hand. "Open up," he said in a deep voice.

Daniel opened the door and let me in. After he shut the door, "I don't like the way he was looking at me," Daniel told me.

I got used to the idea that if a hotel room had a television, there would be no sex.

In the morning, Daniel wanted to stay longer. When I explained that there was only one ferry off the island, per day, he quickly changed his mind and packed his gear. At the ferry dock, he negotiated for passage and blamed our late arrival on me.

["How do you know he didn't murder anyone when you were gone from the hotel room?" the FBI agent had asked. "What about the people in the room next door."

"Because he wanted to stay another night, instead leaving of immediately," I answered.

"Good point," the agent replied.]

We went to Vancouver Island and then went north to take another ferry. This ferry had a narrow passage to pass through. It looked like any false move would make the boat crash. "Whoa!" we both said, as we leaned over the edge of the rail.

"Keep your heads and hands in the boat," the crew said, "We have to keep steady through here."

After we made our way past the rocks, it was open ocean. There was no land in sight. We both managed to keep from getting seasick. The dark green water lapped against the sides of the boat as we picked up speed. The wet air smelled like salt. The dark gray clouds reminded us of the possibility of precipitation. But there was no rain. The crew instructed us to go below deck into our cars.

Vancouver, British Columbia – June 20, 1984

We drove from the ferry to Vancouver, British Columbia, Canada. The date was June 20, 1984. At the hotel, valet parking was included. We arrived at our room. In a short time, the toilet was clogged, and I contacted the main office for assistance. Daniel had me call. He didn't want them to know it was his mess. When the maintenance man arrived, Daniel said, "I don't like the way he was looking at you. You're just wearing that ugly pink skirt," he complained.

The pink skirt showed off my 19-inch waist and flat abdomen. I knew I was supposed to look at my own actions, but how could he marry me and be so disinterested. I told myself I had to change my expectations. "I'll change for when we go out," I said.

"What?" Daniel asked. He seemed to awaken from a stupor.

I answered, "I'll change clothes for when we go out. I'll wear pants if that's okay." It was the only remaining nice outfit that I packed for the trip. I avoided packing clothes that might wrinkle.

Daniel left the room to go downstairs. When he came back, he said with an airy breath of exertion, "I asked them where our car was located, and they told me." He was carrying all the items from the trunk. For no rational reason, Daniel cleaned out the trunk of the car including all of the camping gear, while grumbling at me. "Why did you pack all this stuff?" he asked with wide-eyed irritation.

I complained, "First, I'm punished at Sol Duc for not packing enough, now I'm criticized for packing too much". This was on top of the fact that I didn't want the responsibility of packing his things and mine.

Daniel made sure to bring in the thermos that had gelatinous goo dripping out of it. He pointed to it with his index finger, tapping the side of the thermos, "Make sure you take your drink."

I looked around at the shallow sink in the bathroom and the bathtub and found no place to sterilize the thermos. The hotel water did not run hot enough for sterilization and the thermos could not be submerged in running water. I decided it was best to use the hotel glasses.

Daniel complained, "We'll have to pay for that!" He indicated the hotel would charge a fee for the use of the drinking glasses. I rolled my eyes.

"Hey look," Daniel said. "I just opened up the fridge. Let's eat in here."

I picked up the hotel price list and read the prices out loud. Did he expect that the items in the fridge would be free, but that I would need to pay for drinking water out of the glass?

Daniel shook his head, disagreeing with the prices. He closed the fridge and then reluctantly put back the bottles of alcohol lying on the bed that he had already taken out.

I picked up a brochure for local restaurants. There were plenty of places to eat near our hotel. After all the driving, I was ready for a nice walk. I looked out the window. The weather was wonderful, only a few clouds, not too hot, and no rain. The sidewalks were clean, wide, and inviting along the storefronts with attractive and colorful signage.

Daniel shook his head and enthusiastically pointed to information in the Yellow Pages about a restaurant just outside of the city. I complained about more driving and the possibility of not being able to find the place. He argued that it would be easy and just off of a main road. I reluctantly went along with his choice. We went to a German restaurant in Richmond, British Columbia near the international airport. It was June 20, 1984.

We were quickly taken to an available table. The waiter led us to a dark brown wooden table for two. He turned around and with a gesture of his right hand beckoned us to sit down. The waiter returned to the lobby.

Daniel took hold of the back of the chair facing the lobby, remained standing with a smile, and waited for me to sit down.

I thought Daniel was playing the gentleman, waiting to sit until after I sat down. I reached for the vacant chair, which faced the wall, and pulled it away from the table. I sat down in the chair, put down my purse, and organized my silverware in the proper order. Glasses with iced water were already on the table.

Daniel watched me sit down, walked towards the lobby, and then left for ninety minutes.

I assumed Daniel went to talk to the waiter in the lobby. I waited to order until he came back.

The waiter kept coming back to ask me, "Are you dining alone?"

I asserted, "No, I am waiting for my husband." I wasn't dining alone on our honeymoon. And Daniel had chosen the restaurant.

When my husband returned, he stood at the table and looked at me.

"Aren't you going to sit down?" I asked.

Daniel said, "I've already eaten."

I gasped. "You already ate?" I asked. I was crushed.

"I thought you would order without me," Daniel explained.

"No," I corrected, "I was waiting for you."

The waiter gave me dinner to go. The waiter gave me a weak smile and said, "At least he paid for the meal."

I choked out the words, one at a time, "It was my money."

I gave Daniel the money to pay for dinner to save face. I wanted to be respectful. I didn't want to draw attention to the fact that I was raised in a wealthier family. I didn't want to be controlling or in a power struggle. Giving him the money to pay for the meal was meant to be an act of love. Then he used my money to buy a meal somewhere else. His breath smelled like corn dogs.

Why didn't he just let me stroll through the city and eat at a restaurant near our hotel? He left me waiting for ninety minutes. If I was dating, I would have dropped a guy for this, but this was my husband, and the pre-marriage counselor challenged each of us to look at our own actions instead of others.

We went outside. "I'll drive back," Daniel said. He walked around the car and stood by the driver's side door.

The parking lot smelled. I didn't notice it on the way into the restaurant. The scent reminded me of a bad neighborhood. I had no other reference for the odor. I paused and stood still for a moment. Why did he take me to a bad neighborhood to eat by myself, instead of letting me walk to a nice restaurant and enjoy the good weather and colorful storefronts? I was tired of sitting. It was too dark for a stroll through the city. I looked towards the north. The streetlights were on, and the sky was turning dark blue. Over the buildings, clouds strung through the sky like black shoelaces.

A tall Canadian woman with light brown hair came up to stand at my left side and said, "I think the smell is coming from your car." I looked at her, she was a nicely dressed woman holding a plain beige leather purse in her right hand.

Then I looked down at the gravel-paved parking lot, the rocks cemented into the asphalt. The parking lot was on a slight decline. The pavement was dry. There were no spills. Nothing was leaking from the car. I slowly raised my gaze to the blackness of the rear tires, the tires looked like they were washed. I looked at the back seat and the trunk. I turned my head to the left to look at her and shook my head. That couldn't be possible. My husband had just cleaned out the trunk into our hotel room, needlessly so, all of the camping gear and food. The car and the trunk were completely clean, empty in fact.

[Reflection: Where did he go while I was waiting at the restaurant? I didn't notice if he changed his clothes. How am I familiar with the smell of a bad neighborhood? When was I in a bad neighborhood? And when did I smell that smell? Why do I associate that smell, which was actually the smell of the early stages of dead human body decomposition, with a bad neighborhood?]

When Did I Smell That? - Meet Me at the Pier

While we were engaged, Daniel wanted to take me to downtown Seattle. "I want to show you how to walk through a bad part of town," he said. I took my umbrella with me. He coached me to walk with purpose, not making eye contact with anyone. He let me go first, and then he hurried up to walk alongside me.

A homeless man was sitting on the ground in a doorway of an old building. He was covered with a blanket. He jumped in fear when he saw Daniel come up beside me. I felt an odor I hadn't noticed before. I glanced at the homeless man, "A homeless man is sleeping right there," I pointed out. The homeless man slouched back in the doorway and moved his head to the left to watch us.

"Don't point," Daniel instructed, shaking his head. "We leave him alone." I gave Daniel my full attention.

We went to Ivar's Seafood to order fish and chips. Ivar's had a blue and white sign and a charming appeal. We ate outdoors. Blackbirds were at our feet picking at crumbs with their beaks. The weather was warm and sunny. Ships floated on the blue water, under white puffy clouds. The waves of the water made a lapping sound against the pier.

On the second trip out, Daniel objected to me carrying an umbrella, "People will wonder, 'Who is this woman carrying an umbrella on a sunny day?'"

I objected, "It is Seattle. It always rains in Seattle, or nearly so. People are expected to be prepared." But Daniel insistently shook his head.

I left the umbrella at home. I was instructed to walk down to the pier. Daniel planned to come up beside me and we would walk to the pier together. I was less confident without my umbrella, and I walked faster. I thought about the homeless man I saw before and peeked at his doorway. The corner where he slept was empty. I reached the pier before Daniel caught up. I rested my forearms on the railing and watched the colors of the sunset. The seagulls flew past, joyful when they found food. The clouds partially blocked the sun and long shadows stretched across the boardwalk.

When Daniel did arrive, he smelled. It was a heavy rotten cabbage smell, like the one that wafted through the air when I passed the homeless man in the doorway on the first trip, but more pungent and lasting. "You walked too fast," Daniel criticized. He settled into a place next to me by the railing, but he didn't soak in the view.

"How long did you spend downtown?" I asked Daniel, trying to understand the reason for his heavy foul odor.

Daniel shook his head. I wanted to stay until the sun went down over the sound. The colors of the sunset were dramatically shifting from orange and red to deep purple. "Come on before they wonder why we are here," Daniel said.

Is he worried about tourists? I pointed my arm towards the beautiful sunset. It was clear why we were here, enjoying the sights. There was no value in leaving early. The traffic on the freeway would deplete with time, rather than get worse. Daniel ignored my request and led me back to the car.

The police arrived from the north side of the pier and stopped to question a small group of tourists. We were almost to the car and prepared to leave the parking lot before I heard their pursuit.

Later after we were married, Daniel took me into downtown Seattle and showed me the homeless there. "It was explained to me that the mental institutions were too crowded," Daniel said, describing the problem. "So, they put them out on the streets." He encouraged me to look around. "They used to pick them up and put them in jail, but that was giving them a warm place to sleep and a free meal."

I saw the smiling faces of the men standing by and warmly smiled back.

"There are just too many of them." Daniel looked back at me. "You see the problem, don't you?"

I nodded.

"I want to help them," Daniel told me. "Once every other week, stay in Seattle on Sunday after church, and feed the homeless. I'll take them to McDonalds. You can stay home." He had a clown smile while focusing on someone past my left shoulder. He looked down at my face to seek approval.

I thought "feed the homeless" meant he would give them food.

Returning to the Hotel - Vancouver, B.C. June 1984

Daniel drove the car back to the Vancouver B.C. hotel. He said, "I'm going to take the scenic route." He drove past old-style Victorian homes. The night was becoming darker and snuffing out any light. Tall evergreen trees looked black against the dark blue sky. The road was winding and without street lights. It dipped low, then went high again with more curves, the way a road does when it follows a river.

Only a few houses had porch lights on, making the scenic road seem pointless. "I think this trip would be better in the daytime," I said. I looked over at Daniel, who kept his eyes on the road and carefully watched the speedometer.

Daniel didn't respond. He continued driving forward until he found a small road that veered off to the left. He gave a sigh of relief when he spotted it. He pulled into the smaller road and turned a sharp right to park. "Don't get out of the car," he said, "The car is on a ledge. And don't move."

I was exasperated. I assumed that he tried to turn around and misjudged the landscape in the dark. I sat still in my seat. I could hear the flap, flap sound of his canvas tennis shoes running on the pavement. He opened up the trunk. I heard the heavy breathing sounds of exertion. I felt the car heave forward. I placed my hand on the dashboard and remembered those cartoons of when people are on the edge of a cliff and the car is about to fall off. I thought that I should move to the back seat. I looked behind me. I saw Daniel to the right rear of the car.

I heard the sound of something heavy dropping on the pavement. Daniel must have found a large rock to keep the back tires from rolling forward. The rock made a loud thud and then a soft thud. I envisioned a dense rock with ridged edges, 2 feet across and 2 feet high for the weight. I imagined the rock black, because a porous rock would have broken apart when it landed and made a crunch sound. He should move the rock in front of the tire instead of behind. While this thought was in my head, I heard the flap of his tennis shoes. The car was steady now.

He came to the driver's side door again. He looked up and paused before assuredly lifting the door handle to re-enter the car. He turned the key to start the engine and put the car in reverse. I expected the car to run over the large rock that he dropped, but we smoothly went past. Soon we were back on the highway.

"I wouldn't have been able to do that," I said, looking back at the place in the road. It was hard to see it. There was no turn out. I wondered, "Where did we turn around?"

"Right," Daniel answered with a smile, "You wouldn't have been able to do that."

Daniel drove the car down the highway back to the Vancouver B.C. hotel and refused the valet service, which was prepaid. When he returned to our hotel room, he went straight into the bathroom. I hoped he wouldn't plug up the toilet again. I didn't want the embarrassment of calling the maintenance man a second time. And I'd be expected to call. I was the one who reserved the hotel room. The hotel had rented to me. Isn't that why I was delegated these embarrassing tasks? The sound of the shower answered my question, and I was relieved. But it was our honeymoon. Couldn't we shower together? Couldn't we walk up to the hotel room together? Why couldn't we eat dinner together?

I leaned my back against the edge of the counter. Then I turned to the left and spotted our bottle of champagne. Daniel wanted to drink before we left for the restaurant. He had grabbed those small bottles of alcohol out of the refrigerator and tried to stash a couple into his pocket, before realizing that we'd have to pay.

Daniel came out of the shower and sat down on the bed.

"We could drink the champagne," I reminded him, reaching over for the bottle, trying to forget being stood up for dinner on our honeymoon. At least we could share a drink. I held out the bottle, ready to pour into the glasses.

Daniel shook his head and paused. He stared at me.

I asked, "Isn't that why you brought the champagne out of the trunk?"

Daniel frowned as if he was silently reprimanding a child who misbehaved.

Had he already had a drink too? Without me? I held back tears. I told Daniel, "I tipped the valet." I didn't care if this news irritated him. I wanted to irritate him.

Daniel was angry with me. He stood up and got up close to my face and demanded, "You could give me money," he said. "I'm the one who parked the car."

"I hadn't asked you to park the car," I argued. "The valet service was paid with the hotel reservation." It gave us an opportunity for more time together, and he dodged it.

I didn't understand why he did the things he did. Why completely unload the trunk, if he wasn't planning to drink the champagne? Why stay in a nice part of the city and not enjoy walking through it? Why did he insist on driving to a bad part of town to eat dinner, if he was planning to leave me alone at the restaurant to eat by myself? Why not use the valet service that was already paid for? I foot the bill for the wedding, and I was footing the bill for this honeymoon. I deserved answers.

Daniel walked past me back into the bathroom. He was cooling down his anger and putting cold water on his face.

It seemed that at every possible moment, Daniel avoided spending time with me. For ninety minutes, I waited for him to come eat with me. And this was our honeymoon.

At least he didn't toss me out of my own hotel room like he did at Orcas Island. I gasped. That was only yesterday! So much has happened since then. I forgot it was only yesterday. Wasn't there any day of our honeymoon that was good? On our wedding day, he didn't allow me to have any of the wedding cake and refused to make love to me at the hotel. The next day he was angry at me for not packing my college backpack for hike-in camping and refused to make love to me again. On the third day, he packed up the tent before I had a chance to get dressed and had me take a ridiculous scenic route. On the fourth day, he destroyed my pictures of the deer, watched me as I became frustrated at the scenic viewpoint, and locked me out of my hotel room.

I sat down on the edge of the bed, put my hands over my face, and cried. I used facial tissue in an attempt to control the smudge of the mascara, but it was hopeless. Why did I try to use mascara? It was a guarantee that I would cry. My nose was stuffy, and I used the tissue to clear it.

When Daniel came out of the bathroom, he looked at me, stopped short, and then glanced at the hotel room door. He wondered what the hotel staff would think. He made of change of direction and knelt down next to the bed. He looked intently into my face. He started to kiss me gently. He put his hands on my freshly shaved thighs and looked softly into my eyes. He leaned forward and whispered, "Nothing," into my right ear. Instead of whispering "sweet nothings," as most people do, he took the phrase literally and made it into a joke.

I wasn't laughing. The point of "sweet nothings," was to provide compliments and set the other person at ease. Simply saying the word, "Nothing," didn't qualify as sweet, no matter how it was said. But at least he was trying.

Dan started to kiss me on the lips. His nose wasn't plugged. Although he kissed me gently, because I was crying, his kisses prevented me from being able to breathe. This asserted a different type of control. It seemed as if too often, Daniel would kiss me when I was crying.

Not being able to breathe, prevented the passionate kisses I fantasized about through my teenage years. I gave a sob, grieving the death of the passionate kiss that I dreamed of receiving. The inhale of air made my nose fill with fluid. The plugging of my nose made it even harder to breathe. I told myself that this was a new experience, a real experience, and to enjoy it.

Dan pulled back the bed sheets on the right side of the bed. He had me lie down and took off my clothes. He took off his own clothes.

This process seemed more natural than the awkward time in Anacortes. There wasn't an uncomfortable time of deciding what goes where. Although now the top of my head was hitting against the headboard with each thrust. I winced.

When he finally stopped, he arched his back away from me. Then he stood up and said, "Lie still. Close your eyes."

I obediently lay still with my eyes closed. I suddenly felt cold, it felt as if he turned up the air conditioner. I opened my eyes, expecting to see him at the room temperature controls. But he hadn't moved, he was standing over me, holding the blanket up, looking at my naked body, studying my flesh, and looking away at the empty space next to me on the bed. But it wasn't a look of admiration. He was comparing me to someone or something, and I wasn't measuring up.

The headboard at the hotel was smooth and made of dark walnut wood. I pointed to the headboard and explained that the top of my head was hitting against it. "If you don't stop that, I'm going to get brain damage." It was a small thing we could improve on, not too much to ask, I thought. Making love would get better with practice.

Daniel looked at the headboard with affection and gently smiled. He went into the bathroom.

I obediently lay still. I didn't put my clothing back on. I thought he might join me in the bed later.

Daniel redressed, sat down in the armchair, covered himself with a blanket, and went to sleep there, leaving me to sleep alone on the queen-sized bed.

In the morning, I showered and got dressed.

Daniel said, "You can drink from your glass now."

I looked at the glasses and his smile. Already I spotted it when he made a tense smile. I learned that one on our first date. I switched the glasses so that my glass was in his position and his was in my position and then watched to see his reaction.

He stepped back just slightly in alarm. Then he watched and waited until I was around the corner and brought out both glasses with water in them. He sat down in the chair that he slept in. Then he drank water from his glass and smiled contently at me. With a nod, he indicated an invitation for me to drink from my glass.

I refused my glass of water. I was used to practical jokes, and I wasn't falling for this one. I went without a drink of water for a long time after that, but I managed okay.

Daniel frowned in concern. He took back the glass of water and dumped it, looking over his left shoulder at me with irritation. He grabbed up our luggage to take it out to my car.

I checked out of the room. The hotel staff verified the contents of the refrigerator, looking for additional items to charge to my bill. They noticed the armchair was slept in. "We can always tell," they said.

"I apologize for any damage to the chair," I stammered.

They kindly said, "It's alright. We just wanted to know if you were okay."

Daniel met me outside the hotel. He had thrown all the food into the dumpster when he cleaned out the trunk. He said we could stop at a grocery store on the way to camping.

British Columbia, Canada – June 21, 1984

It was June 21, 1984. We drove to a wildlife safari in British Columbia, Canada. I admired the black panther, who is a black spotted leopard. He was so pretty with a glossy black coat. His eyes were blue in the center with yellow around the rim. The eye colors were a beautiful contrast to the black fur. I looked closely, and I could see his black spots in the black fur. Yes, he was a leopard. I smiled at the impressive creature.

The black-spotted leopard looked straight towards me. His pupils dilated. His eyes turned black to match his fur. He took an angry dive. He started to pace along the chain link fence of his cage. He walked back and forth the full length, abruptly turning at each corner. The zookeeper said, "If there was an exit in the chain link fence, he planned to find it or create his own." I wondered if they were feeding the poor cat. I stood still and leaned towards him, trying to assure him I wasn't a threat, trying to understand his reaction.

The zookeeper yelled, "Get out of here."

I reluctantly walked away towards the next exhibit. The zookeeper mounted the chain link over a building inside the cage and tried to restrain the angry cat.

The leopard didn't calm down. He looked back and up at the zookeeper and then determinedly looked forward. He dived at the front of the cage. He expected the zookeeper to release him. He thought the zookeeper came to be a partner in his escape.

"You think it's her?" another zookeeper asked. He came to assist and viewed the situation, "I think it's him." He pointed to a tall placid man three exhibits away.

Daniel turned his head towards the zookeepers and watched with a non-plussed expression while the two zookeepers partnered in restraining the cat. One shower wasn't enough to stop the leopard from smelling what Daniel had done the night before. Instinctively the wild cat knew something was terribly wrong.

I walked on and looked at the hippopotamus. The hippopotamus leaned over and opened his mouth wide for a mouthful of fresh grass. He showed off a large row of teeth and tongue mostly covered in dark green pre-chewed plants. Later the zookeeper approached me, "You need to leave," he said kindly. "It isn't you, it's him." I nodded. He explained, "He is stalking you and it is riling the animals." The zookeeper wasn't talking about the hippopotamus. I tried to drink this in. The zookeeper referred to my new husband who appeared to stay three exhibits away from me. Annoying, immature, unromantic, and disconnected, but not troublesome.

The zookeepers continued their conversation a distance away, "He's dangerous and the animals can sense it," the second zookeeper said.

"Shit yeah," answered the first zookeeper who tried to calm the agitated black spotted leopard. "We'll have the authorities take care of him."

I went to the dirt parking lot, to the driver's seat of my car. I glanced down at the tires that were clean last night, but muddy today. I waited. My head was down in disappointment. This hadn't gone as I had planned. I promised myself to try to have a good day. I rested my forehead on the steering wheel. I wasn't sure what to do.

Daniel stood still. He quietly and intently watched me. Then he walked over to my passenger-side door, opened it, and climbed in. I started up my car and drove away.

The zookeepers were shocked into silence. "Well, we knew he was here with someone," one of the zookeepers said. The comment was meant to jolt them out of shock. They turned to stare at each other.

I drove on to the Canadian-U.S. border. We switched drivers there. Daniel said I wasn't good at answering questions when we passed through customs, so he answered the questions while I stared forward. After we cleared Canadian customs, we switched drivers again.

I stopped at a grocery store for food. I bought food for smores. "It will be fun," I insisted. Daniel couldn't talk me out of it. I also bought fruit. Daniel dodged to the left and selected two muffins for our breakfast. We purchased the items. We drove to a remote camping location and parked in the lot. This was a hike in camping. The outing was selected by my husband.

I had an opportunity to decide where to stay the first two nights (Seattle and Sol Duc), then he had an opportunity to decide for the next two nights (Anacortes and Orcas Island), then I had an opportunity to decide (Vancouver, B.C.), and now it was back to his turn.

"Do I need a parking pass?" I asked Daniel.

"No," Daniel said. "The car will be fine." We packed gear on our backs, a tent, sleeping bags, and necessities. We walked over red rocky hills. The rocks were twelve to eighteen inches across and slid under my feet. Twice I had to steady myself with my right hand and stop to rest. We hiked through a narrow path and green ferns. The floor below us was soft with pine needles. It had more cushion than a track made of recycled rubber tires. It was comfortable for my feet and a pleasant contrast to the red rocks. The air smelled of green plants and distant berries, not huckleberries, something woodsy like salmon berries. Insects buzzed past but did not bite or become a nuisance. It was too early in the year for mosquitos. The forest was thick and there was no place to pitch a tent. We walked on to see light gray rocks. We crossed over the rocks of a dry riverbed to a flat place to pitch a tent nearby.

Daniel looked around the corner and through the trees. "There is another group of campers through there," he said. A short chuckle escaped from his mouth.

"Do you want to go to a different location?" I asked in a quiet voice.

"No," Daniel answered. "This is fine."

The tent was pitched over round gray rocks. We didn't bother to stake the tent. We set up our sleeping bags. The small amount of food we packed in was secured inside the tent. "Save it for the morning," Daniel said.

It was the longest sunlight day of the year. We didn't converse much. When the air turned cool with a gentle breeze and the night sky turned dark gray, we retired into the tent. I lay in my sleeping bag. Chipmunks scampered up and down the sides of the tent. We didn't make a fire, so roasting marshmallows for smores was skipped.

Daniel observed, "They smell the graham crackers and are trying to find the entrance."

"Should we leave some crackers out for them?" I asked.

"No," he said, "It would just attract more pests."

Daniel rolled over restlessly and then got up to leave the tent. He tapped the side of the tent twice, which scattered the chipmunks. He unzipped the tent door open to leave and then zipped the tent door closed. I heard his first three steps on the gray rocks. Then there was silence.

The wind pressed against the sides of the tent, and I began to feel chilled. The tent rain flap grabbed gusts of wind and coughed them back again, filling and collapsing in rhythm. I gave up waiting for my husband and forced myself to sleep. I rolled onto my side. The gray rocks shifted under my weight. It wasn't uncomfortable.

I saw Daniel return to the tent in the light of early dawn. He was gone for six hours. I record the time when people start to annoy me. When he arrived back at the tent, he didn't have an odor and may have showered.

"Did the chipmunks keep you awake?" I asked him in the morning.

"They were squirrels," he corrected. "And, no, actually I thought they were cute." He smiled.

There wasn't much food to prepare for breakfast. I looked for a spigot, a water source.

"Look around you," Daniel said, pointing to the dry river bed, "There is no water."

[Reflection: Daniel let me think there wasn't a water source. He didn't want me to have contact with the other campers.

After I divorced Daniel, I took another camping trip. I asked someone, "Is that a chipmunk or a squirrel?"

He answered, "It's a chipmunk," and he explained how to distinguish the difference by looking at the markings on the tail.

It was as I thought. "Are there squirrels that look like chipmunks," I asked, just to verify.

"No," he answered. "There are just chipmunks."

Daniel was attempting to make me doubt reality, letting me think I couldn't even tell the difference between a chipmunk and a squirrel.]

"Let's break camp," Daniel said. He prepared the gear for transport while I got breakfast ready. I turned around and was startled to see the tent and sleeping bags rolled up and secured onto his backpack. This time, I was somewhat prepared. I changed my clothes first thing before leaving the tent.

We munched on the muffins for breakfast as we hiked out. Before we reached the red rock hill, I heard a loud roar. "What was that?" I asked. I looked back towards the forest.

"Something angry," Daniel said in a definite tone.

"A bear?" I asked. Daniel seemed to nod.

"Keep looking and moving forward," Daniel instructed. "Don't run, walk quickly, and don't stumble" Daniel commanded. This was good general advice.

I'd never felt so frightened. I might blame Daniel for riling another animal, but the sound was more than a half mile away. He wasn't anywhere near it. When we reached the red rocks, two hikers started their journey on the trail, a young man and a woman. "A bear," I told them. They smiled. "An angry bear," I clarified. They continued forward without slowing pace. It was surreal.

"Just keep walking forward," the instructions came from behind me. The other couple walked past. When we reached the parking lot, Daniel said, "We made it."

I turned to look at Daniel, expecting him to be looking over his shoulder, worried. Instead, he was standing tall and had a strange, satisfied smile on his face.

At this hour there were only about five cars in the parking lot. My light blue Nova was about ten parking spaces down.

"That's them," the hiking couple we passed earlier said to the ranger. The young woman was pointing at us.

"I'll let you drive," Daniel said. I stepped into the driver's seat and started to roll down the window. "Keep your window up," he said. I put my keys in the ignition and placed my car in reverse.

"He had her drive," the ranger pondered with a frown. "Why did he have the nervous one drive?" Something about this scene seemed off.

"I just wanted to know what they saw," the ranger explained.

"She said it was a bear," the female hiker said.

"That wasn't done by a bear," the ranger said.

Daniel curled up in the passenger seat and immediately fell asleep. I drove south through Everett and on to Seattle. I looked for a place to stop.

"Don't stop at a hotel. They will ask us where we came from," Daniel said.

What a weird thing for him to say. "We came from Kent," I responded.

"Oh, right," he said, "We came from Kent." He smiled contently.

I stopped in Tukwila. I hoped to find a bathroom. Daniel shook his head and drove us home.

At the Seattle First United Methodist Church, the women assured me that all people have problems on their honeymoon. We needed to work through it. The church was a large two-story building. It had a domed roof that used to be glass. The dome was plastered over and painted in pastel blue designs, similar to the Sistine Chapel. At noon the sunlight illuminated the paintings. The lower floor was used for coffee hour. It had brown carpet, a gym area that was also used for dances, and a large industrial-sized kitchen.

That evening, I made smores in the microwave, but Daniel dashed off. He had the neighbor lady tell me that he doesn't like smores and stop offering them to him.

Her husband said, "Would you stop getting into the middle of their arguments?"

I told her, "You can help me with this." I showed her the thermos Daniel gave me and complained to her, "The cork has something like mold or bacteria in it that won't go away, and I can't sterilize it out."

She looked at the door, "Does he drink from the thermos?" she asked.

"No," I said. It was a good question. Why didn't he drink from the thermos? Why did he want me to drink from the thermos?

Without touching it, she gave the thermos a close inspection. "Throw it away," she advised. "The thermos lining might be cracked. It might not just be the cork."

"The thermos lining," I said. "I hadn't thought of that."

Later Daniel asked, "Where is the thermos I bought you?"

"I threw it away," I told him.

"You threw it away?" Daniel complained.

"You never drank from it anyway," I reminded him.

"I paid for that," Daniel said in a higher pitched distressed tone.

A thermos from a garage sale? He paid for what? Did he pay extra for the old thermos or a cork that stays infected with bacteria?

When we visited my parents, I told them about the bear at the campsite.

Daniel shook his head and told them, "I didn't see a bear."

I nodded and explained, "We heard a bear." I looked at Daniel who showed no recognition. "I heard a bear," I corrected. "And a ranger came out."

Daniel said, "There was no ranger."

I looked at Daniel and partially said and partially asked, "Only other campers." I tried to reframe the event. The man who wanted to question us wasn't a ranger, as I supposed, only another camper, and possibly the one who roared in anger. There was an uncomfortable silence.

My mother came to talk with me, "He told us that you didn't go camping."

"You mean the final night," I clarified.

My mother shook her head, "He told us that you didn't go camping."

I said, "He told you we only went camping once."

"No, he said you didn't go camping at all. He only said you went camping once. Because he felt sorry for you. He said you went straight from the hotel in Seattle to the ferry in Anacortes and then stayed on Orcas Island," my mother said.

"He's saying that we went straight from Seattle and then stayed the night in Anacortes?" I asked. How could he skip the camping? The mother deer with her fawn nibbling on the leaves. The walk down "Lover's Lane." It hadn't been as romantic as I hoped, but still.

"He said that you didn't stay in Anacortes, you got straight onto the ferry from Seattle," my mother said.

I wondered if there was a ferry out of Anacortes that late in the day. From the schedule, it looked like there was only one ferry from Anacortes to Orcas Island. I was sure of it. We would have needed to leave Seattle at three in the morning to catch the only ferry. Daniel was not an early morning riser. The hotel checkout would have been slow. While I calculated the times in my head, my chance to respond to my mother's comment had come and passed.

My mother shook her head to correct me, "From Seattle, you stayed two nights on Orcas Island, and then two nights in Vancouver B.C."

"That only adds up to five nights," I said. "We were gone for six nights." Math would save me.

"You stayed two nights in Seattle," my mother said.

"We didn't stop in Seattle on the way home," I reminded her.

"No, you stayed two nights in Seattle before leaving for San Juan Islands," my mother said.

Daniel told a different story. He gave my family the impression that I was dishonest, had a poor memory, or was mentally unstable. I assumed he wasn't very bright. My parents assumed I lied about taking camping trips. But camping was one of the things Daniel and I had in common when we decided to get married.

Daniel stood in the family room doorway, listening in on my conversation with my mother.

I looked at Daniel and told him, "We stayed a night in Anacortes. Remember the bathtub that looked like it was the right size for turtles?"

Daniel shook his head and gently smiled like he was correcting an amusing child. He slowly turned and went back into the dining room to talk to my father.

Daniel confided in my father, "I only married her out of obligation. Because I felt sorry for her." That day is when the defamation started, earlier than I expected. Already he was planning something.

[Reflection: My father didn't tell me what Daniel had said until close to the time of Daniel's arrest. There were decades of psychological manipulation during that delay.]

"You're trying to figure out what he is doing," a dinner guest observed, as she sat down next to me on the sofa. She understood my facial expression more than my parents.

I shook my head. I'm not going to change my story for a moment. Why would anyone believe Daniel instead of me? I've always told the truth. I have an excellent memory. He's just playing another childish joke, like the one at the tourist viewpoint on Orcas Island.

"I made the itinerary," I answered. "I know where we went."

"Maybe he's describing the honeymoon he wanted to have," the dinner guest suggested.

I walked out into the dining room, where Daniel was talking with my father, "Next time we go on a trip, we'll spend two nights in the same spot," I reassured Daniel. I was appeasing, or I sounded like I talked to a child who needed to be consoled.

Father said, "Hmmm." He was thinking. I assumed he supported me, and wondered about Daniel.

[Reflection: Over time it was clear that my father believed I was crazy. My mother believed I was a coy actress making up stories. Fortunately, the FBI assures me that hotel records are kept for many years. "They go back a long way," the FBI agent said. "And because you always made the reservations, the trips would be easily verified." Thank God!]

Psalm 10: 7-11

"7 His mouth is full of curses, lies, and oppression. Beneath his tongue lie trouble and wickedness.

8 He hides in the shadows of the villages, waiting to ambush and kill the innocent in dark corners. He eyes the weak and the poor.

9 *Ominously,* like a lion in its lair, he lurks in secret to waylay those who are downtrodden. *When he catches them,* he draws them in and drags them off with his net.

10 Quietly crouching, lying low, ready to overwhelm the next by his strength,

11 The wicked thinks in his heart, "God has forgotten us! He has covered His face and will never notice!" ~ from *The VOICE*

I looked out the sliding glass window at the upper pasture. I told Daniel, "I want to go to Jesus Northwest. There will be performances of Christian bands coming up in July. There will be camping at the Clark County Fairgrounds." I smiled with enthusiasm and nodded. Excitement had me at the edge of my seat. He could make this up to me.

Daniel said, "Who is camping?" He looked at my parents, with his eyes, but kept his head facing forward towards me. He had a weird smile on his face. There was a hushed silence.

I explained, "The audience is camping. They camp in the grassy area next to the fairgrounds. It will be fun and my first opportunity to go. We both like Christian music and we both like camping, so it is perfect!" I expected this idea to sell. I wasn't questioning what I remember about our trip, but I was starting to question my ability to influence others.

Daniel looked at my parents, smiled, and shook his head, as if to say, "See what I mean, she is crazy." My parents remained silent.

Later, I asked my parents, "He told you that he doesn't like to go camping?"

"No," my parents said, "He said that you can't do camping."

A man at the Seattle First United Methodist Church sat down across from me at the coffee hour after the 11:00 service. The brown carpet muffled his steps as he walked over, but he dropped his body down into the chair with force. He wasn't planning to be ignored.

I drank a glass of lemonade while sitting on the black leather sofa in the multi-purpose room. I told him about the events of the honeymoon and the conversation Daniel had with my parents. This was weighing heavy on my mind.

The man informed me, "The ferry transfers would have been unavailable at that early hour. To take the Bremerton ferry out of Seattle, you would miss your connection with the ferry to Orcas Island."

"Isn't there another way? What about going through Tacoma and over the Tacoma Narrows Bridge and then travel north?" I asked.

"That would take longer," he said with a smirk. "You would probably need to leave your Seattle hotel at two or 2:30 in the morning to catch the only ferry to Orcas Island."

The hotel check out would have been slow or unavailable. "I needed to use the counter check out for my hotel discount," I recalled

He nodded, "Was there ever a time that your husband put something in the trunk?"

"Put something in the trunk?" I asked, "Or take something out?"

"Either one," he shrugged. He looked at me intently.

"There was the time Daniel nearly drove off a cliff. He had to get out to adjust the car," I answered. I shook my head, not as a "No," but because the situation was disorienting. I was sure the rock should go in front of the tire.

"Did he put something in the trunk or take something out?" he asked.

"Let me think," I responded. "I put my hand on the glove compartment when the weight of the car shifted," I thought about the way the car heaved forward, as if we were losing weight from the back end. I said, "The front of the car seemed heavier. He took something out of the trunk."

"I think he was doing something wrong," the man replied.

"Something …?" I asked. I was a newlywed and didn't consider that my husband could do anything wrong.

"I mean," he explained, "If he put weight into the trunk, it would have provided more traction for the back tires. And it would have been easier to back the car out."

I responded, "The car has a rear wheel drive."

"Even more so," he said with a smile.

[My thoughts reflected on my new husband's poor mechanical skills. What I needed to think about was the fact that he could do something wrong. I shouldn't idealize him. I also didn't consider that the trunk was completely empty at the start of the trip and there shouldn't have been any weight to unload.]

The man at the church coffee hour said, "I didn't come here to have a conversation with you." He stood up and walked behind me to have a helpful conversation with Daniel about the mechanics of tire traction.

Shortly after I was scolded for talking about the scenic route. I assumed Daniel was embarrassed, but I agreed to never mention it again.

The next week at the coffee hour, the man sat down across from me and told me, "I believe you. I mean I <u>COMPLETELY</u> believe you." He put his hand out in emphasis. His straight brown hair was tousled from worry. "Now we need to figure out what he removed from the trunk." He looked down with a concentrated look. But I was out. I wasn't allowed to talk with him anymore.

[A new thought: If Daniel wasn't turning the car around on the scenic route. How did he know of this place, unless he was there before?]

Holes in the Wall– My Childhood, April 1983

The situation with my parents was already strained. I left home at seventeen in the middle of my senior year of high school. I came home from school and found holes in my bedroom wall. My first thought was the red woodpeckers in the cow pasture that visited the walnut trees. I imagined them flying around in my room. My bedroom window was closed. Maybe my mother opened the window while I was gone.

When my mother returned home from work at the library, she was tired and stressed. That morning my father wanted her to leave for work an hour early to impress her supervisor, but the plan hadn't worked. I brought her upstairs to my room to see the holes. She looked at the holes and then looked at me, very angry. She accused me of taking a gun and shooting holes in the wall.

I took a closer look at the holes. They seemed too high up on the wall to be done by a gun.

"You stood on a chair and shot holes in the wall," my mother accused.

I turned around and looked at the only chair in the room, an unstable chair. It was part of a school chair and desk set from when my grandmother taught third grade in the old school house in South Dakota. No one would stand on it. It had a curve in the seat to accommodate a child. If these were bullet holes, the person would need to move about the room while shooting a gun.

My father came home from work. He was also tired from a full day at work. He came to look at the holes. He confirmed that they were bullet holes. He disagreed that a person had moved around the room while firing a gun. He said, "No, a person stood in one place and shot all three holes like this." He demonstrated shooting the northernmost shot first and then rotating counterclockwise to shoot the remaining bullets toward the west and south.

"That story you told about birds in your room is just ridiculous," my mother scoffed. She thought I was playing coy and using advanced acting skills.

"But someone in my bedroom with a gun would be okay?" I asked. Had the world gone crazy?

I left to stay the night at a friend's house. I didn't know what to do, but I couldn't sleep there anymore. "Triangulate the shots," the friend's father said.

I had no idea what that meant, so he explained. I went back to my parents' house, stood on a stable chair, and measured. The shots did triangulate to one point. The shot to the south was up at a higher angle than the ones to the west and north, which were steady. The shooter had to be six inches taller than me or 5'11". The chair would put a person too high.

"The first bullet deflected. He was learning how to use the gun for the shot to the south," a high school friend suggested. "After that, he was steady for the remaining shots." This theory suggested a teenage shooter with an unfamiliar gun. There was a group of boys who were recently expelled. They sold stolen guns. One of the boys had a reward for his capture. In my perspective, he became a key suspect.

The local police suspected my father. "He is the one who had access," the police officer said. They wouldn't do anything, because it was his house. "He can shoot up the walls in his own house if he wants. There is nothing we can do about it."

The high school counselor placed me with a foster family. I had told him, "Sleeping in the woods with the coyotes howling is less frightening than sleeping at my parents' house where someone is shooting a gun." Just before I graduated from high school, the foster family arranged for me to stay with Liz.

Later I discussed it with a Washington State Assistant Attorney General. His afro hair was cut short, and his skin was the color of burnt chocolate. I wonder if it is prejudiced to describe the color of someone's skin as a dessert food. He was dressed in a dark gray pin-striped business suit. He said, "No, his baby daughter's room is shot up and he doesn't rise to his feet to run upstairs? I don't care how tired he is." His tie, in an expert Windsor knot, was tilted at an angle across his chest.

"You mean, it was my father," I clarified.

The assistant attorney general nodded with certainty.

"How did he know where to shoot to avoid the electrical wires?" a man at a coffee shop asked. "Was it just dumb luck? My point is it had to be your father." He leaned back with confidence and smiled, "Does that help?" He expected me to have a look of relief.

I didn't. I left. How could any father do that?

[Reflection: Later my father confessed to the shooting, "I realized what I was doing." The bullet to the south was the last bullet he shot. The bullet's deflection was caused by hesitancy, as he decided to stop.

Karen Roberts

After years of defending my father and then discovering that he was responsible all along, my mother resigned to say with a shrug, "He likes to intimidate people."

Later two social workers discussed the case, "He shoots up her room, and then he decides that she is the one who is dangerous. That is incredible. 'Smelling a rat?'"]

Japanese Art - Daniel's Childhood 1968

Futakuchi-onna was a Japanese monster who had a mouth in the back of her head. She was portrayed in art and as a character in a movie. The Japanese stories were told to teach ethics and morals. One effectively "kills" the monster by avoiding the immoral and unethical behaviors that create them. Daniel's oldest brother had purchased the video cassette a year after the movie's release in theaters. He introduced Daniel to the movie. The brother used the television as a tool to keep his baby brother out of his hair, while he played video games in his bedroom. Their father worked at the post office and their mother brought home extra income for the family.

The cartoon frightened Daniel as a child. His mind dealt with the fear by attempting to desensitize, creating an obsession. He watched the 1968 movie over and over again until age ten. The repeated exposure method was unsuccessful in drenching his terror. Daniel finally conquered his fear of the monsters by telling himself it was just fantasy; it wasn't real.

"The Japanese produce the best art," Daniel told me at his parent's house when we were dating. "And the scariest movies." He asked, "Have you seen them?"

"Do you mean Godzilla movies? Godzilla and the giant moth?" I asked. The early Godzilla films had a reputation for looking like small toys manipulated for the screen. Often because that was exactly how the movies were produced. The moth looked like a real moth, which was exceptionally creepy.

"No, movies more realistic than that," Daniel clarified.

"Right," his oldest brother interjected with sarcasm, stepping away from the television set in the living room, "Because cartoons are more realistic." His grin broadened across his face.

"You never should have had him watch that movie," their mother scolded, as she emerged from the kitchen.

"That's right," Daniel gasped, turning to look at his brother, "It was you who got me watching it." His oldest brother was one that Daniel admired.

"It kept him occupied for hours," the older brother said in his defense. "Why couldn't he tell the difference between cartoons and reality?"

"At that age, he just couldn't," their mother said. She gave a quick glance at Daniel and then looked back at her oldest child. Their mother complained, "His sister would do things with him." She expected more from his babysitting and gave him an accusatory look, "You know I had to work."

Her oldest son said with sarcasm, "Right. Work." There was a chilly silence that followed. Daniel looked at his mother with an odd smile.

"That work," their mother said, pointedly "Paid for your video games."

"I'm well aware," the brother said in a deep voice. Their mother went back into the kitchen.

"Was work at the church?" I asked. "Custodial work? Cleaning the bathrooms?" My mother volunteered to clean the church and dragged me along. I hated waiting while she cleaned the men's restroom. I imagined the older brother having to wait while his mother cleaned the women's restroom at the church.

"She didn't clean the bathrooms," Daniel said. He made a disgusted face and looked at his brother. My guess was met with silence. There was tension in the room.

The older brother played video games to escape the reality his brain refused to process. As a teenager, he was old enough to grasp the situation. "Which bedroom was yours?" I asked him as I pointed towards the hallway. I was trying to picture the events in my head.

"It wasn't in this house," Daniel corrected. "It was in California."

The older brother leaned slightly toward Daniel's ear and said in a hushed tone, "She's starting to put things together. Psst."

But he was wrong. I was missing the nuances of the conversation. For some reason, guilt came to mind. The older brother immersed in video games to escape the uncomfortable feeling of … guilt. My thought wasn't fully formed and was cut short.

Daniel and I stepped out of the house. I took another look at the seafoam green home painted in 1978. If they had Halloween decorations, they were taken down. I looked around the neighborhood. It was one of the few houses on that street without decorations.

Daniel's Adolescence - 1978

In 1978 to invoke stranger danger, Daniel's father told him about John Gacy, the Killer Clown. Daniel was 17 years old at this time. His father figured he could handle the story about a man who sexually molested little boys and buried bodies in the crawl space.

Gacy murdered his first victim in 1972 and at least thirty more after his divorce in 1976. He met his victims while working as a clown. His last murder of a teenage boy led to Gacy's capture in 1978. His conviction for thirty-three murders was the most homicides in United States legal history. Gacy was sentenced to death by lethal injection on March 13, 1980. At that time, the death sentence was delayed by court procedures.

Daniel's only tool to deal with fear was to try to desensitize. This method hadn't worked with the Japanese monster movie, and again it failed with the story of John Gacy. The repeated exposure created an obsession with the Killer Clown. Unlike with the cartoon, this time Daniel couldn't tell himself that the monster wasn't real.

To calm him, Daniel's parents took him to the upholstery store. They wanted to see what colors produced an emotional response. This was the beginning of color therapy. They tried a variety of pastel colors. They expected pink would do the trick, but it definitely did not. Pink was the color of a horse drawn by Japanese artist Takehara Shunsensai who showed the animal swallowed whole, testicles and all.

Daniel's mother said, "Seafoam green was the only color he responded to." Daniel's parents spent thousands of dollars to make everything seafoam green in an attempt to calm their youngest son. They painted the exterior of the house seafoam green with white trim and received compliments from the neighbors. They painted the interior walls seafoam green. They purchased a sofa that was seafoam green. They had an armchair specially upholstered because none could be found in seafoam green. The floor was carpeted in seafoam green. The cushions of the dining room chairs were seafoam green. Daniel's brother called this, "The seafoam green explosion."

Their car exterior was seafoam green. When this was not enough, they searched hard for a car that had a light green exterior with a matching leather interior. And then as a final touch, the steering wheel was wrapped in light green leather.

The seafoam green was a double-edged sword. The hue, although it appeared to calm Daniel, was the same color as the kimonos of women in Japanese art. This included Futakuchi-onna's kimono in the 1841 drawing by artist Takehara Shunsensai. But creating a monster and then destroying that monster doesn't kill the original monster, it only creates another monster.

His parents' search for a matching interior and their purchase of a light green Toledo, did nothing to stop Daniel from committing his first murder. The first victim was riding in the passenger seat of the Toledo when Daniel decided, "I knew I could overpower her in the water," of the Green River. He planned his first murder while surrounded by the color of seafoam green. The year was 1982, four years after his Killer Clown obsession began.

In 1987 another victim would be forced to swallow seafoam green colored pills and drink seafoam green swirling fluid, as Daniel stood over her. This deadly combination was given to his girlfriend who performed fellatio. He extended no affection in return after her request to leave the relationship.

Returning to My Apartment- November 1983

Daniel stepped away from the house at a brisk pace. He walked me home and shook his head. "To my brother sarcasm was a gift. Don't read too much into what he says," Daniel explained. We walked past the Halloween decorations that remained on the houses. "Should we tell them what day it is?" he asked with a grin.

"Why do people decorate with orange and purple on Halloween?" I asked him as we walked home. Fallen leaves crunched under our feet. The autumn leaves were falling faster than the neighbors could keep up with their rakes. "Why not orange and black?" I wondered aloud.

"Black isn't really a color," Daniel explained. "It is the absence of color."

I turned to look at Daniel. "No black isn't the absence of color," I argued.

"Sure, it is," Daniel asserted, leaning forward and looking back to make eye contact with me as we walked.

"Black the combination of colors," I insisted. I remember creating black in an oil painting class. The art teacher insisted that we mix our own black, instead of using black from the tube of paint.

"White is the combination of colors," Daniel informed.

"If you mix paint together," I insisted, "You don't get white!" This seemed obvious.

"Black is the absence of colors," Daniel insisted, "And white is the combination of colors. Look it up!" This was a textbook response.

"But why purple?" I asked, "Is it because purple is the closest color to black?"

"I'm wondering," Daniel said, "Why green?"

"Because green is the color of witches," I answered.

Daniel looked confused and shook his head, "No, green isn't a witch's color."

"Green is the color of their skin," I clarified.

"Dead bodies have light purple skin," Daniel suggested. We were approaching my apartment complex now. "I always thought she would look better in light purple," Daniel murmured.

"Who?" I asked. His comment seemed random.

"Futakuchi-onna," Daniel answered.

"Is that a college friend?" I asked. I wondered if this was someone at the college dorm. I realized, with disappointment, that I didn't know Daniel's college friends, only the friends from church. I was completely open with him, and he seemed to have a hidden world.

"No," Daniel said in an irritated tone, "Never mind."

"Light purple is lavender," I told him.

Daniel disagreed and insisted, "Light purple is just light purple." He stopped short, "Why do you always have to argue?" I was on the sidewalk to my apartment at Briar Crest. He turned to leave and said, "I rarely have a chance to see my brother," Daniel complained, "With him living in California. And I had to cut the visit short to walk you to your apartment."

"You didn't really need to walk me home," I countered.

"He told me to," Daniel explained. This is what his brother whispered in Daniel's ear, when all I heard was Psst.

"I am perfectly capable of walking by myself."

When I returned to my apartment, I asked Liz about light purple.

Liz was sitting lengthwise across the sofa with her head buried in a book. A pillow cushioned her back. The afternoon sunlight from the picture window was her reading light. She didn't turn to face me when she answered my question. However, she agreed with me, "Light purple is lavender." Her response was automatic. Liz aspired to be a country singer someday and studied music production at Green River Community College. I retreated to my room to let her study.

Later Liz asked, "What was the conversation we just had? I have a feeling it was important."

"I asked, 'Light purple is lavender, right?' and you agreed," I reiterated.

"Oh, okay," Liz answered, "It was nothing then. I mean nothing important."

Character Play – Summer 1984

We sat on the loveseat in the living room area of the studio apartment. Daniel said, "Comb your hair over your face," handing me a comb. "Now look in the mirror," he said. "It looks like your head is on backward," he said with a soft chuckle and pleased smile, admiring the reflection in the mirror. "Now, part your hair in the back," Daniel instructed. He wanted me to look like Futakuchi-onna.

I reached for a rat tail comb to part my hair down the back.

Daniel continued to admire the morbid sight in the bathroom mirror. "A person can't turn their head that far, not even a dead person. I've …" He stopped short and paused.

I quickly turned my head to watch him speak. Was he about to say, "tried"?

For a brief second, I imagined him turning the head of a dead girl, with light purple skin and dark brown hair, to see if her head rotated backward. Bits of mud and decomposed leaves were stuck to her staring face. Fog subdued the dim street light, the river bank, and the sound of flowing water at his right side, as he kneeled over her lifeless body. Fulfilling his sexual need without her objection.

Light purple is how he described the skin color of a dead person on our first Halloween when he walked me home. I had a feeling there was someone at the college dorm, someone who tied these conversations together. He was someone I should know about, but couldn't see. Months later, I was no closer to gaining more insights.

I didn't want to put the conversation at Halloween in 1983 together with this summer 1984 request for character play. That couldn't be right. My imagination was running away with me. I turned my head forward and frowned at the mirror in front of me in the bathroom.

"An owl can't either," Daniel continued. "It looks like they can, but their head doesn't go all the way back."

Changing to the new topic of birds and animals, "That is an interesting fact about owls," I praised with admiration. I enjoy conversations about nature. That must be what Daniel meant to say. My hair was parted lengthwise down the back. This wasn't pretty. He wanted my hair parted horizontally across the back, but the part didn't stay that way.

Daniel frowned in disappointment but accepted the uncompromising effects of gravity. He nodded. "Comb your hair over your face and wait for me like that when I come home," he requested.

"No," I answered. I put down the comb on the counter next to the bathroom sink. I was willing to play dress up, but not this. This was out of my comfort zone. Why was this a turn-on? If he thought my face was pretty, why would he want me to cover it up?

Daniel's smile melted off his face. He reached for the comb and looked down at it with regret.

I explained to him, "It is a rat-tail comb, and the handle can be used to part the hair."

Daniel laughed and repeated the term, "Rat-tail." He raised his gaze in consideration,

I explained, "I don't like my hair parted down the back. It doesn't look good that way. And my opinion matters too." I stepped out of the bathroom.

"A friend of mine said to work with my situation. I thought this would be an improvement." Daniel admitted, "I don't like the color of your skin."

I sat down on the bed and looked down at my bare legs. "I could go tanning," I offered.

"No," Daniel disagreed, "That would put it in the wrong direction."

"What color is my skin?" I asked. I wanted to know how he saw it.

"It's beige," He answered. He took the comb and left the apartment.

"You gave him an answer he didn't think possible," a neighbor told me. "You need to have more imagination. It would give the two of you a chance to play dress up," the neighbor said with a smile. He hoped the suggestion would be enticing.

I explained what Daniel asked me to do. I only said that Daniel wanted me to comb my hair over my face and then sit and wait like that for him.

"No," the neighbor said and paused to take a breath. "He wanted you to play dead?" He looked away, and then he left the apartment. Maybe the neighbor identified something that I didn't.

At the daycare, I asked Bonnie, "What color is beige?"

"Less yellow than tan," Bonnie answered, "Lighter than brown."

"How is my skin the wrong color?" I asked Bonnie. Creamy beige. I always thought my skin color was pretty. I was proud of it. "I've never been told that my skin is the wrong color before," I confessed.

"Look around you," Bonnie said. Dark brown industrial carpet spanned the floor. Cream-colored walls framed the room. Artwork was scattered about on the walls. Children bustled around the room.

The room had children with brown skin, yellow skin, white skin, Cambodian, and African. Is their skin the wrong color? What does that even mean? Each of them might view their skin color as beautiful. An African American boy, with dark brown skin, climbed into my lap. I gave him a kiss on the upper forehead at the hairline. My upper lip grazed his kinky black hair. I put my arms around him and gave him a hug. He let me carry him into the lunch room, where I served the food.

After work, I had a question, "What color should my skin be?" I asked Daniel.

"Light purple," Daniel answered.

"From Finland?" I asked. "No, that's blue tone. Which nationality has purple-tone skin? Do you want to date another Norwegian?" I looked at him with expectation. At least that would make sense. "You want to date someone like your father?" I asked. That didn't make sense. I frowned, "Or like your mother?"

Daniel looked away, "It doesn't have anything to do with my mother." He moved away from the bed and went back into the living room area.

At the church, we had coffee hour downstairs. I asked a young married couple, Karen One and her husband, "People from Finland have blue-toned skin. Who has purple-tone skin?"

In our young married group at Seattle First United Methodist church, you had a good chance of guessing the name right if you called a woman Karen. This was a popular name for girls born in 1965. The name landed right for the young married group. Karen One was the first Karen to join the group. She was tall and slender with short brown hair. I was Karen Three. There was a Karen Two, but she didn't come to the church as regularly. The pastor for the young married asked me if I wanted to become Karen Two in light of the other Karen no longer attending. I declined the invitation in case Karen Two decided to return to the church.

"Suffocated?" Karen One's husband answered. He had blonde hair and a wide frame in contrast with his wife.

"No," I said in a frustrated voice. "You don't understand. Purple-toned skin. The way some people have yellow tones, red tones, and brown tones. Africans have brown-tone skin, Asians have yellow-tone skin, and Native Americans have red-tone skin. Purple tone."

Karen One's husband thought for a moment and then firmly answered, "Suffocated."

Daniel ducked out the back of the church on the north side and was now in front of me waving his hand wildly for me to come.

"He went all the way," Karen One's husband paused as he traced Daniel's path with his eyes, "around the building."

"Don't go," Karen One requested. She didn't want me to answer Daniel's beck and call.

"He wants to talk to me," I recognized Daniel's urgency, "I'll be right back."

Karen One's husband looked back at Daniel, "I don't like the way he was looking at you," he said to his young wife.

"At me?" Karen One asked in alarm.

"Yes," her husband answered with a frown.

"We are leaving," Daniel said, pulling me towards the west side of the building.

"I wasn't done with my conversation," I objected.

"Good," Daniel said. We parked on the east side of the building and never used the exit to the west. Until then, I hadn't noticed the exit was there. Even though we were in the basement of the church, the hill was at such a slant that there were another six steps down to street level. We quickly and silently walked around the building towards the south, and back to the car.

I remembered a movie where a person was suffocated with extra pillows on the bed. I checked the bed when we arrived at home. There were no extra pillows.

"What are you looking for?" Daniel asked. I turned to look at him and wondered why I couldn't check the bed without him watching. I don't remember my answer.

Later that summer, I became very ill. I was projectile vomiting yellow fluid. The 24-hour call nurse decided it was bile from liver breakdown. She thought my husband worked in a morgue and had gotten me sick. The disease was not common. She instructed, "Drink water to flush it out of your system." She urged, "Don't let him near you unless he is washed up."

"I'm going to have to leave you for a while," Daniel said. I wasn't sure what a while meant, but he was gone for a little over a month. I internalized this as a failure. I failed as a wife.

One last attempt at camping - late Summer 1984

Daniel told me that a new REI opened up in downtown Seattle, so we went to check it out. There were zero-degree bags and sleeping bags that kept you warm to zero degrees Fahrenheit. There was polypropylene, a material that whisks away moisture better than wool or cotton. There was a variety of cooking equipment. I insisted on buying a soup mix for us to cook over a campfire or stove. Daniel settled for a package of warm wool socks.

"We had a grand opening a year and a half ago," the REI cashier said. He wondered why Daniel picked now to go. But he was cheerful and didn't complain about the extra business.

Daniel had a different plan for a camp stove. We went to Fred Meyer and bought a small stove that took butane fuel canisters. He explained how the canisters work. He bragged about the safe design, how it could tip over and not create a fire, unlike kerosene.

Daniel found a campsite northeast of Seattle. Not a state park. Just a small campsite with a gravel parking lot nearby, separate from an RV lot. I cringed a little when he showed the campsite in the AAA handbook. I preferred to stay at state parks and in places away from RV lots. Yet, I agreed with his choice.

After we arrived, Daniel unloaded the trunk to our campsite. He insisted. It was a welcome change for him to take care of this himself, instead of insisting that I help pack it in.

I asked Daniel where the restrooms were.

Daniel pointed to the other side of the parking lot.

I didn't see the outhouse at the parking lot. Instead, I saw the RV area. I took a deep breath and decided to enjoy the walk. There was mowed grass and a narrow dirt pathway to the RV area. There weren't many birds or small animals. The RV campers brought their pet dogs.

When I arrived, I asked about restrooms and was told, "There is a restroom for the tent campers."

"Well, while I'm here," I asked, "Can I use the restroom?"

"Sure," a lady said with a smile, drying off her hands with a paper towel from the dispenser on the wall. She tossed the paper towel in the garbage can and left the woman's restroom with two of her friends.

On the way back, a man pointed to the outhouse near the parking lot entrance. There was no running water to wash our hands. I nodded, but I was a little disappointed. I returned to the camping area from my nature walk. I found a water spigot closer to our tent site. I filled a pot with water and then prepped the butane camp stove. I poured the soup mix into the pot of boiling water.

Daniel came wandering past and his body swerved to the left. The pot handle was bumped and the water and most of the soup spilled out into the ashes of the fire pit. It was odd. He had no reason to walk in that direction.

"I have more soup mix in the package," I informed him. We weren't in a hurry, I started dinner early, and this accident was not a loss. But Daniel insisted on leaving to buy food.

When he came back it was becoming dark. He had to go bags with greasy hamburgers and fries from a fast food place for our dinner. He explained why the burgers were cold. He had to drive an hour and a half to find a food place. "It was the best I could do," he shrugged.

I would have preferred the soup, instead of greasy burgers and stale wilted fries. The fries were dry and hard to swallow. The cheese melted on the meat and down the sides of the bun. The bun was greasy and moist from soaking up the hamburger oils. It was as if the meal was made hours ahead of the order at a shady hamburger stand.

[Reflection: Later when I described this experience to the FBI, the agent interjected, "Could he have purchased the meal in advance before the trip and kept the food in the trunk? You said he was the only one who unloaded to the campsite."

"Oh, yes," I answered, "He could have. What an odd thing to do."]

I turned to look at Daniel. He was standing to the right of the tent, just out of view. He told me, "Keep turned around". I assumed he was taking a leak next to the tent, and turned my head to look away.

I didn't smell hamburgers and fries on his breath. I don't think he had any. Or he brushed his teeth when he showered. When did he shower? He seldom showered, and he smelled like soap.

[Reflection: Now I wonder if he left brown colored spots on the ceiling of the shower at the campsite. Bright red spots that fade to brown and then to black. After the divorce, I found these spots on the shower ceiling in my house, when Daniel broke in to steal food.]

After eating I left the campsite to wash my hands at the spigot and use the restroom. I returned and I could hear the gravel from the parking lot crunch under my feet with each step. It was harder to see, now that the sky was becoming darker. The gravel terrain let me know that I was still in the parking lot. A policeman came up on a motorcycle, "Did someone call for a cop?" he asked.

"No," I answered. I saw him speed off.

At the campsite, Daniel criticized, "Did you wash your hands before you used the bathroom?"

"I had to," I answered, "My hands were greasy from the hamburger."

"But at least you ate," Daniel boasted at his provision.

"I saw a police officer in the parking lot," I informed him, "He asked if anyone called for a cop."

Daniel argued, "A police officer wouldn't refer to himself as a cop."

"Well, this one did," I countered. I was becoming tired of these interruptions in my view of reality. While Daniel went into the tent, I sat out under the stars and listened to the silence. I hoped for some sort of clue. Everything was pitch black.

Daniel came out of the tent insisting, "We need to leave." He packed up in the middle of the night. "Saves us from trying to figure out what we plan to do for breakfast," he said. We had plenty of food for breakfast, warm and cold food. But Daniel wasn't going to allow an argument.

Daniel said. "And in the morning you'll need to try to find the restroom again." He made a horrified face, with his eyes wide, his mouth open, and his jaw dropped down to the left. "There were all kinds of complaints about you using the wrong one."

"I'm fine," I said. I didn't need to use the restroom. I already peed in the pitch black dark, next to the tent.

Daniel looked down on the ground, where I had peed. "I said I don't want any litter, and I meant it," he scolded. It was okay for him to take a leak there, but not me.

[Reflection: I think he was stuffing clothes into his overnight bag. And then he unzipped the tent and threw the bag in. I had assumed he was taking a leak.]

I drove out of the campground. On the way out, I saw an ambulance flash overhead lights. Two rangers came out to give the ambulance driver instructions. The driver quickly turned off his overhead lights and then turned off his headlights.

"Whoa," Daniel said. He sharply turned his head to look to the right.

I thought Daniel was looking for the road and couldn't see it. "I see him," I answered. I could see the vehicle in the dark. I drove around him and continued down the narrow, paved road.

[Reflection: Daniel wasn't looking for the location of the road, as I originally assumed, the turn of his head was too far. He was looking at the location of where he buried the body. He wasn't expecting the body to be found so early.]

The next morning, I received a telephone call, "Do you know why I'm calling?" the police officer asked. My name was on the camping reservation.

"No," I answered, confused.

"You left in a hurry last night," the police officer said in a gruff voice.

I answered, "I hoped if all we planned to do was go camping, then the trip would be successful."

The police officer said, "Oh." He hung up.

After I hung up the phone, Daniel approached me from across the living room and asked, "Did you tell him you were camping alone?"

"No," I said. Why would I tell him that? I wondered. I don't see a reason to lie. I turned my head and looked at the phone, wishing the police would call back. I didn't know which jurisdiction was calling, and I didn't have a way to return the phone call.

"I'm not going to go camping with you again," Daniel said, wide-eyed. "That was the last time." He turned away from me.

Daniel wanted me to do laundry after we got home. I had done laundry before we left. "You know, because we went camping," he said with a shrug.

We hadn't gone camping for more than a few hours, and Daniel's clothes were filthy and encrusted in thick dirt. I guessed he did camping things while I was away from the campsite. My clothes were basically clean. I hesitated to wash them together in the same load. It would take an extra wash to remove the mud, and my clothes would come out dirtier than they were now.

At church after the social hour of coffee and cookies, I mentioned the incident at the campsite. "He didn't want to eat the soup," a church woman interjected. She was insistent that this was the correct answer, but this was only part of the problem.

The focus on the soup interrupted my thought process and didn't foster my instincts. While Daniel was gone to pick up the greasy burgers and fries we didn't need, a tragedy happened. If he bought the fast food ahead of time and placed it in the trunk, there was plenty of time to shower.

He didn't smell when I ate dinner. And he smelled like he had eaten beforehand and brushed his teeth.

The next Sunday I talked to Karen One about the dirt on Daniel's clothes. "You'd think he spent time on the camping trip digging," I said, complaining about the crusts of dirt on his clothing.

"He's a trench digger?" Karen One asked.

"What?" I asked.

"Never mind," Karen One answered, "You said, 'it looked like he spent hours digging.'"

Karen One left with her husband. "What is a trench digger?" I asked. The question seemed important. I didn't have a way to look up the term.

Daniel approached me and said in a shocked tone, "You won't need to do my laundry anymore."

I should feel elated at the thought of doing less laundry, but his statement is more of a cut. I felt betrayed by the previous conversation.

"Why did you tell him what I said?" I asked Karen One at church the next Sunday.

"I didn't," Karen One answered, "Why is he listening in on your every conversation? Is the better question."

I couldn't find the new butane camp stove again. When I asked Daniel about it, he looked at me, hit me hard on the face, and said "Stop being stupid."

Later at my parent's house, "I had to hit her to knock sense into her," Daniel defended himself.

My mother asked me, "Is there any time you were away from the campsite?"

"When I left to use the restroom, he directed me to a different campground, one with RVs, and then said that the campers there had complained about me using their restroom," I answered.

"And this somehow got back to him," my mother said sarcastically.

"I'm telling the truth," I objected. Although there was no way anyone at the RV campground would have known where I camped or would have been able to complain to Daniel.

"No, Karen," my mother said, "We believe you."

"I think he did something," my father said. He approached closer and looked concerned.

"He wanted you to go to another campground," my mother said, thinking aloud, "so that you wouldn't run into anyone from your own campground and get into a conversation with them."

"I never saw anyone from our own campground," I admitted. It was weird.

My mother nodded. But this might be the last time she believed me.

[Reflection: While I'm following my nose, and the lack of smells, it is first, and certainly not least that I remember one of our nights at the apartment in North Queen Anne in February 1984.]

North Queen Anne - February 1984

I asked Daniel to contribute to the bills, even if it was just a little it would help. It was too much for me to pay the rent and feed the two of us. I was only eighteen years old. I lost my job caring for an elderly woman with cancer, and I hadn't budgeted for the expenses of two people. Daniel hadn't helped me keep the job. He called and requested that I leave work that evening for a movie at the theater. I asked Daniel to look into receiving a donation of food or money.

Daniel took a bus downtown. He said, "The man I spoke with told me I wasn't someone for that group."

This frustrated me. "I'm going to call them and make a complaint." We needed food and help just as much as anyone else.

Daniel admitted, "I never stepped off the bus. I saw the homeless people lined up around the block for a handout. I stayed on the bus and continued traveling forward." He expected me to understand.

I took a deep breath and pressed my lips together. I couldn't think of anyone more worthless.

A housemate was downstairs dropping off his laundry. He rented a room on the main floor.

I asked him, "What do you think Dan meant when he said, 'You are the first live woman I've slept with.'?"

"The women he sleeps with are usually dead?" the tenant asked.

"I think he is referring to pornography," I replied with uncertainty.

"Blow up dolls?" the housemate asked with a laugh. He laughed, "You'd better check the closets for blow-up dolls." He gave a humorous side glance as he passed through the hallway. Then we walked away, back up the stairs to his room. He shook his head and continued to chuckle.

I didn't know what blow-up dolls were. I assumed he was referring to dolls that explode. I shuddered. I waited to gather my courage. I carefully opened each of the closet doors, taking care to be gentle in case the doll was triggered by movement like a hand grenade. The last closet door I tried was the door in our room for the closet Daniel promised the landlord he would never open. When I opened the door, it wasn't a closet at all. It was a door to the outside. There was a stepping stone path that led to the front sidewalk. The stones were sparsely surrounded by mowed grass. Rose bushes that lost their leaves stood waiting for winter to complete. They weren't in the best of care, but someone pruned them.

I waited until Daniel was home to ask him about the door to the outside. "I'm sorry I opened this closet door," I apologetically explained. "I noticed the door isn't a closet. It leads to the outside."

Daniel paused and was silent. He stared at the closed door and then admitted, "I knew about the door to the outside, but I would prefer if you use the main door." He said something about the lock. Then he added, "We can leave by this side door," Daniel explained, "But let's always return by the main entrance. So, that the other tenants see when we return." He looked at me to make sure I agreed.

I didn't understand the reasoning, but I agreed to this rule. Daniel went upstairs. When he came back downstairs to the room, he was cross at me for asking the other tenant about what he said. "Don't tell the other tenants what I say to you," Daniel complained, "I had to lie to him."

My legs dangled over the edge of the bed and my ankles were crossed. My back was hunched over, and my head was down. I was buried in my textbook. I struggled to memorize the Latin words. I was sitting on the upper bunk bed studying my anatomy and physiology book. In class we were learning the names of the bones in the human body.

"I didn't think it," Daniel said in awe after he walked through the apartment door. The words on the page blurred. I barely looked up other than a glance to verify who was talking. "Because we are in the basement," he finished his sentence. "But there is a crawl space. There is plenty of room under there."

I expected his next line to invite me to come and see. I was aggravated at the interruption to my studies. Instead of inviting me, he disappeared again. This time he was gone for a while. This met my needs, so it didn't concern me. It was peaceful with him gone for a couple hours. It gave me a chance to read. Later in the night, when I was mostly asleep, I saw Daniel slide out the side door. I heard him but pretended to be sleeping.

When Daniel returned, he used the same side door, violating his rule. He slowly rotated to close the side door. He walked straight through the room. He was hunched over while crossing the room from the side door to the bedroom door. He was at nearly a 90-degree angle so that his torso was almost parallel with the floor.

I looked at his facial expression expecting to see nausea or pain. It was dark in the room, but I could see his eyes. The dim light in the room reflected off his eyes. He was facing forward with a pleasant expression and looking at the door in front of him. He didn't look to the side or to the floor. He exited the bedroom door towards the laundry room. But he didn't go into the laundry room. That would wake another tenant who shared the basement.

When Daniel returned, he ducked down to go into his bunk. I turn onto my side in my bunk to face the wall. Daniel became startled, stood back up, and stared at me for a long time. He was also loudly sniffing me. This was very uncomfortable. I tried to lay still and did not move a muscle. Finally, he turned and climbed into his own bunk.

The next day I asked him, "Are you feeling nauseous?" I hoped to understand why he was hunched over.

"I'm fine," Daniel answered with a soft smile. He told me, "I had to convince myself it was okay for you to move." He said this to explain why he was startled when I rolled over in bed.

I asked the tenant who shared the basement, "How did you sleep?"

"Fine," the tenant answered with a cheerful, well-rested demeanor. He was a large man with curly hair, who kept *The Complete Library of Anal Sex* at the head of his bed. I avoided going in there.

The next day it stank. It wasn't the same musty smell of the laundry room. Something more pungent. I sprayed Lysol to kill any bacteria that might be causing the smell. I sprayed it through the air. I used half a can.

Daniel stood and watched me spray the Lysol. He did not step in to help. Instead, he seemed fascinated by the accomplishment. He took the can and sprayed some more. Then he sprayed two cans of Lysol. The Lysol barely took the edge off the smell.

We moved out. I just wanted to move away from there. Kent was a safer community. But the problem followed me. After we moved out, the landlord refused my security deposit. The landlord telephoned to complain to me. He said, "The smell was not better after I spent three days airing out the room in the dead of winter."

[Reflection: This was the worst smell of them all. Two cans of Lysol couldn't douse it. The odor lingered heavily for days even in open winter air. The lingering stench was worse than it was when Daniel dug up and reburied his first kill.

When Daniel was hunched over, he was carrying a dead person on his back. There is no other explanation. When Daniel returned to the bedroom, he didn't have an odor. He must have showered between dropping off the body in the crawl space and returning to the bedroom to sleep. I didn't hear digging. I'm not sure that he buried it.]

Beaten to Light Purple – September 1984

Pastor Lowell Murphry provided our pre-marital counseling, and he was in charge of the Sunday School at Seattle First United Methodist Church. Daniel and I signed up to teach the middle school students. Or rather, I pleaded with Daniel to sign up with me as Sunday School teachers; and Daniel gave in. In my mind, I was doing this for him. From his perspective, he was doing this for me. I hadn't taught a Sunday School class before. I was sure that I could do it, but I was very nervous and fretting. I looked up to Daniel as the older, more experienced, mature Christian counterpart.

I prepared blueberry pancakes as a Sunday morning treat. Daniel told me that he enjoys a champagne breakfast with Belgium waffles topped with fruit and sprinkled with powdered sugar. He liked to dine fancy and pretend that he was rich. The closest I could get to this was my father's favorite berry pancakes, which we often made with fresh-picked huckleberries from an outing to Mt. Saint Helens. Daniel never had them made from scratch.

The trick was to thoroughly mix the pancake batter until it is velvety smooth and then gently fold in the berries to prevent them from bursting and releasing juices into the batter before frying on the griddle. The berries absorb the heat, so care needs to be taken to ensure the batter is cooked through and not burnt. The first two blueberry pancakes turned out good. I continued to fry up the full batch.

"What happens when you break them up like this?" Daniel asked. Before I could stop him, he aggressively stirred the batter.

"No! You get purple ..." I yelled. "Those will be your pancakes."

"I wanted a champagne breakfast, and you make pancakes," Daniel said.

I gasped. Preparing these took skill.

"Let's see how it looks on you," Daniel said. He went to the other side of me, took the light purple pancake batter, and dumped the whole bowl down onto my head. The pancake batter stuck into my eyelashes and made it hard to see. The batter dripped down my face. Batter went into my nostrils when I tried to breathe.

Daniel grabbed a wooden spoon from the kitchen and slammed it down hard onto my head. The strike broke the spoon. I fell to the floor with a thud, thud, first my knees and then my hands to break my fall.

"God!" Daniel yelled, "Anyone else and that would have knocked them out." He wasn't apologetic for striking me. He was surprised and disappointed that I didn't have a concussion. "The bowl absorbed the blow," he calculated.

I crawled along the carpeted floor along the sofa towards the far wall. Maybe if the neighbors were home, they might hear me. But, no, they were gone this morning. My only plan was to escape, even if I had to crawl to the outside door.

Daniel held me down by sitting on my back, forcing my body down to the floor. He continued to sit on my back for hours until he was certain that I wouldn't call the police. He called Pastor Lowell Murphry from this position and told him, "You know how it is with newlyweds." He gave the pastor the impression that we were having spontaneous sex. That was so far from the truth.

When I completely agreed not to call the police, he finally let me up.

"Can I call my mother?" I asked. "This was her skirt, and I don't know how to clean the pancake batter out of it."

I wore a 100% wool red, white, and black plaid skirt with pleats. Pancake batter went down my red and white striped soft knitted cotton sweater, onto the wool skirt and my white nylons. The skirt was my mother's and was not washable fabric. I could wash the cotton sweater in the laundry, but not the wool skirt.

I had gotten up early and given myself plenty of time, but after this, I didn't have time to clean up and change clothes before Sunday School started. The thought of taking Daniel with me to teach the class no longer came into my thoughts. I was their teacher, not him. It was a shift of perspective. I looked up to Daniel before this, seeing him as mature. I no longer viewed him as more mature.

"Just wash it," Daniel said impatiently.

"Look at it," I said, holding the skirt out. "It is 100% wool with pleats. My mother wore this skirt to high school in the 1950s. It can't be put into the laundry."

Daniel said, "Okay." And he continued to watch me closely.

I called and explained the situation with blueberry pancake batter on the 100% wool pleated skirt and received cleaning instructions. She didn't pick up on a larger problem.

I sat down on the loveseat and started to pray. I prayed silently, but fervently.

Daniel took a light blue pillow and hit me in the head while I was praying. Light blue, a color of calm. While I was silently praying!

I looked at Daniel, who smiled in triumph. I heard a still voice in the wind speak, "I see you." I closed my eyes and prayed again. This time, knowing that God sees me, and He had a plan.

Daniel turned away and left the apartment.

After this, I just felt marrying Daniel was a mistake. A huge mistake. And that feeling never left.

In the One Bedroom

We moved from the studio apartment to the one-bedroom. The move was necessary from Daniel's perspective. Later I learned that the neighbor saw Daniel bury a new shovel under bags of garbage in the dumpster at the apartment complex, and reported this to the manager. The neighbor insisted on moving to a new apartment without notice or penalty. The management agreed. This was the same neighbor who coached me to fight back.

On the day of the shovel burial, in the parking lot, the trunk of the car smelled of an unidentified smell from a distance of six feet or more. The odor was heavy and carried its own presence like an angry spirit hoping to grab the attention of anyone who walked near. Although the odor didn't linger longer than the smell in North Queen Anne, the fragrance was definitely the most repulsive. And my car was parked only three parking spaces from the white-painted staircase to the second-floor apartment. I would later learn this was late-stage dead human body decomposition.

On that day I stood with my gallon of milk in my left hand and stared at my car, which was borrowed without my permission just one hour short of qualifying as grand theft auto. Missing for 23 hours, instead of 24. Stolen to commit a crime that I couldn't prove. I stayed home to time the length of the theft; my clock and my diligence were my only defense. I smelled the rank odor. I glanced down at my gallon of milk, and I was thankful that I walked to the grocery store. The smell would pass, eventually, mostly. But the stir from the neighbors about the shovel remained for years.

[Reflection: The riverfront property was purchased for development to become a golf course. The body Daniel dug up and reburied would be found by the police a short time later. Daniel was the real River Man, swimming the breaststroke up and down the Green River with a shovel tucked into his pant leg.

Gary Ridgway, called The Green River Killer, never swam the river. Daniel was tasked with burying the bodies murdered by Gary, his drug dealer.

Most of the bodies were Ridgway's kills, but not all. Daniel didn't limit his victims to prostitutes. The man who left to buy groceries was Daniel's kill. The girl who was put in the car with him was only the first girl to walk by.

Daniel had no other reason for his comments to me and no other reason to make my family believe I was crazy for saying the man who crossed West James Street existed. The investigator lost track of what was true and who was truthful. And it was a bad time for the U.S. authorities to forget the true character of their murder witnesses.]

The Fox Trot

The young adult pastor at our church encouraged us to attend a 1940s-style dance. At first, Daniel declined, but the pastor assured him there would be a dance instructor and everyone would be at the same skill level. Daniel saw my excitement at the opportunity to go dancing and agreed. We dressed in 1940 attire. Daniel wore a pin-striped suit from the 1940s that he borrowed from my grandfather. I wore a 1940s dress, hat, and spike-heeled shoes that I borrowed from my grandmothers. I found cotton tights in light beige. The dress was dark green, tight, and short, representing the time when fabric was rationed during the war. A small green handkerchief extended out of the front pocket.

When my grandmother handed me the dress, I was standing in her dining room at the old farmhouse. My grandfather joked to my grandmother, "You wore that on our wedding day. Didn't you?"

"Oh stop!" my grandmother gasped and then laughed.

The shoes were black spike-heeled pumps made of the same material used in railroad ties. The hat had a black dome with long peacock feathers out of the side. While we were on the dance floor, facilitators came up to us and asked about our costumes.

Karen Roberts

The dance instructor slowly went over the steps of the Fox Trot, before having us dance to the beat of the music. The Fox Trot is a four-step square. The man leads. He steps forward one step, right one step, back one step, and left one step. The woman follows. If her feet are stepped on, it is her fault, not his.

The lights went low, and the room was dimly lit for added ambiance. Daniel did very well in the 1940s dancing. He never stepped on my toes, and he did a good job leading. We sat down at a table to eat appetizers, after the Fox Trot was done. Couples at the church said the dancing improved their relationship.

The dance instructor asked us to come to the front of the dance floor. We had won the contest for best dressed. The pastor handed me the microphone to say something about our costumes. I motioned to Daniel, but he preferred to stay in the background and let me speak. It was a magical evening.

Daniel avoided dances where there were flailing arms. He wanted people to be as motionless as possible. The orderliness of the Fox Trot was something he could manage, for one night. The next attempt at dancing had livelier music; sixties music, and this was out of his comfort zone.

The next special event at the church was a harvest festival. The young adult pastor helped set up by putting two steel barrels in the back filled with water and apples. "You're welcome to give it a try," he said, "the rule is No hands. It is harder than it looks. You pretty much have to pin the apple against the side of the barrel to grab it with your teeth.

We stepped over towards the barrels and gazed into the watery depth. Our question about hygiene faded, and we were now concerned about whether one of the children would drown. "How deep is the water?" Karen One's husband asked nervously.

"Two feet," the young adult pastor said.

The next Sunday the barrels were gone. We wondered if the harvest festival was successful. We weren't concerned about the number in attendance. When it was reported that there were no unfortunate accidents, we breathed a sigh of relief.

A young woman in her late twenties came in to talk with us. She was slender, and she had light brown curly hair just past her shoulder. Her brother had been missing for a year and a half, and she identified this as the church he had attended.

Daniel said to me, "Go over to her and tell her that her brother went on a mission trip."

I went over to speak with her and asked her about her brother. She said her brother was very smart. She didn't provide a photo. From what she described, he didn't seem like someone who would go on a mission trip.

Daniel chewed me out, "Why didn't you tell her that he went on a mission trip?"

"Because I don't know if her brother did go on a mission trip," I explained, "and I don't want to give her false information." I looked at her with empathy. If I was in her situation, I would only want true and verified information. The last thing I would want is confusion.

Daniel went over to talk with her.

"Does anyone see a problem with this?" Karen One's husband asked the group.

"She didn't show a photo," I said. I wasn't sure who she was asking about.

I saw the concern in Karen One's husband's face and went over to talk with her again, but she was smiling and laughing. "It's okay," she said, "I have the information I need." And then she left the building.

"I shouldn't have had to tell her myself," complained Daniel.

"I don't know of any mission trips," I muttered, as we made our way to the parking garage. If I heard about a mission trip, I would consider whether I wanted to go. He didn't sound like a missionary type. Why was I expected to give her information that I didn't know? But I didn't ask the question aloud. Daniel was angry with me, and I was pushing my luck.

Headboard

In the one-bedroom apartment, the queen-sized bed was set up. Daniel arrived at the apartment with a headboard. It had a wood finish. The headboard Daniel found, had bookshelves across the front with center dividers. He made a quiet comment, "The bookshelf wasn't being used. They'll never miss it?" He didn't explain.

[Reflection: I didn't receive clear information on where the bookshelf came from. Did Daniel buy the bookshelf at a garage sale, as I assumed? Or did he break in and take it from the apartment building we stayed at in North Queen Anne? Was this the bookshelf that stored the library Daniel spoke of?]

I assumed it was a garage sale purchase. It made a lovely place to display our Bibles for late-night reading and early-morning devotion. From that perspective, the furniture piece was a welcome addition. But Daniel had other plans.

Daniel misunderstood my comment in Vancouver, B.C. on our honeymoon about my head banging against the headboard. From his perspective, this was simply the definition of a headboard and why it was given this name. Instead of amending his actions to reduce the uncomfortable experience, he made it a part of sex.

The bookshelf created hard sharp edges. Daniel removed the pillows from the bed onto the floor to give us plenty of room. At first, he slid my body forward until my head slid onto a bookshelf. This caused the back of my head to hit wood. "My head," I said, "The shelf is hitting the back of my head." From my perspective, this was something to avoid.

"That didn't go as I planned," Daniel mumbled. I thought he'd try to keep my head on the mattress. Next, he moved to aim my head towards the center dividers of the bookshelf, so that the top of my head would hit squarely against the hardest and sharpest part of the bookshelf. This was a painful experience. I put my hand up onto the bookshelf to push myself back down. Daniel insisted that I put my hands down. I grabbed a leather-bound Bible to cushion the blow to my head.

It was my favorite Bible in blue leather with an expansive concordance, and it was given to me by my grandmother. The Bible developed a crack down the front, and then a crack down the back. I held the Bible cover together with masking tape. This triggered a conversation about the incident with the music director. She was very sympathetic and suggested that I start further down on the mattress.

I started 12 inches lower but was again pushed to where my head was hitting against the bookshelf edges. If my head slid past the bookshelf edge, into the bookshelf, Daniel readjusted my body so that the top of my head hit against the sharpest part. I tried to start us two feet down from the headboard, and the same result happened. If I managed to get him to stop before hitting my head on the bookshelf, this was a victory for me, but a failure for him.

The music director started to suspect that Daniel was doing this on purpose. My neighbor, who had moved after watching Daniel bury the new shovel, had told me to do whatever I could to defend myself and that I needed to fight back. The neighbor kept in contact with me even after the move and made sure not to be seen by Daniel.

My leather-bound Bible had taken a beating, and I wasn't sure if it would hold together with more abuse. There were multiple cracks in the cover down the front and the back. Daniel blamed me for not taking good care of my books. In any other circumstance, my books are in the best condition. The next time, I grabbed my thicker New Jerusalem Bible, a soft dark green paperback with gold lettering. This was a volume that includes Judith and the Maccabees.

This book choice held some irony. Judith was a Jewish woman who chopped off the head of a rival military leader when Jerusalem was under siege. The Jews displayed his head on a pike. The Maccabees won a war for the Jewish nation, brutally killing the enemy and forcing them into submission; and I'd learn later that they were my ancestors. The wisdom and courage of my ancestors were at my head, both figuratively and literally speaking.

Daniel pulled the New Jerusalem Bible out of the way, "Here let me get this for you," and he placed it back onto the bookshelf. He went back to ramming the top of my head, which was now swollen, purple, and very bruised, onto the sharpest part of the shelf. This was bruise on top of bruise, a one-two punch, which creates permanent cracks in bone.

[Reflection: Later an X-ray of my neck and spine, showed evidence of head trauma to cervical vertebrae C1 and C2 of my spinal column. My skull crashed down towards my spine and the cervical bones moved to accommodate the collision. The base of the skull no longer rested on the axis bone. C2 was shoved upwards past the foramen magnum. Now my neck bones displayed the shape of a question mark. At this time my epileptic seizures worsened into myoclonic convulsions.]

I made a fist with my right hand and punched Daniel hard in the face.

Daniel leaped up from the bed and placed his left hand to his nose. Warm, red liquid dripped down his index finger. He looked at the blood on his finger. "You gave me a bloody nose!" he exclaimed. His eyes were wide in disbelief. He ran into the bathroom to look at the mirror, first one side of his face and then the other, and made certain that his nose wasn't broken. His nose was unharmed. He looked down at the countertop without focus. He wasn't physically hurt; he was emotionally hurt.

The purplish-blue bruise at the top of my head was stronger evidence for the police as to what had occurred. If they had taken me to the emergency room, an X-ray would have painted a clear picture of the reason behind my reaction. But we didn't call the police.

S & M

The next Sunday after church, Daniel complained about my aggression to a young woman. She had fair skin, shoulder-length light blonde straight hair, and a petite and slender build.

The young woman Daniel spoke to approached to have a talk with me. I never saw her before. I didn't know who she was. I explained to her that I punched Daniel in the nose because he was ramming the top of my head into the bookshelf.

The music director came to my right side. She was supportive.

But the young woman was motionless and continued to stare at me.

At this point, I was screaming for the young woman to get away from me, "Stop staring at me," and "Stay away from me."

Daniel was gloating at the psychological abuse. He found another method to inflict pain.

An older man went to talk with Daniel, who told him that the headbanging was a part of sex. The older man stood next to the young woman and asked her, "Why do you continue to stare at her?"

"Are you talking to me?" the younger woman asked him while continuing to stare at me. She never looked away.

"Yes," the older man said, "I'm talking to you."

The younger woman finally stopped staring at me and indicated to her husband that she didn't believe me, "Why would she ....?"

Her husband answered, "He is her husband."

The young woman turned her head and looked back at the older man.

The older man said to the younger woman, "What do you know about sadomasochism?"

The young woman looked down and agreed to leave with her husband. She stayed away from me after that.

These unwanted public conversations about sex were like a second rape; unwanted pain during sex, followed by unwanted indiscrete conversations.

A college friend came up to me, "Oh God!" he exclaimed, "When I told him to whack the back of your head until you form a second mouth, I was just kidding!"

I couldn't think of a more confusing comment. At least he spoke to me, instead of standing there staring, treating me as a person of interest, and waiting to twist my words to use them against me.

When we arrived home from church, I promised to break Daniel's nose the next time he tried that. He might be a sadist, but I was no masochist. I didn't enjoy being hurt. I had no sexual satisfaction from that. I had given Daniel the benefit of the doubt, not anymore.

Empowerment

I was naive, doormat at the start.

Not seeing the evil in his heart.

I maintained my repose.

Bashed my head, punched his nose

Shield the blows,

Bible from my bookshelf

Let me never fully lose myself.

Many pieces that lock into place

In events so dark, that I can't face

Yet it is amazing.

I am alive to sing.

Our mighty, faithful God takes control.

My God receives the credit in full

I am not only writing my song.

The Author is with me all along

My part in God's story.

To give praise and glory.

I'm mortar, that supports the strong wall.

A thread in crocheted lace in a shall.

Our part in God's story.

Karen Roberts

We find hope and joy.

On the Other Side of McDonalds

Daniel portrayed me as the dangerous one. Along with my father taking his gun and shooting up my bedroom and letting my mother think I was the one who did it, this character profile stuck. My mother believed Daniel and my father; and because she claimed to know me, others believed the false character profile too.

[Reflection: I would go 18 months without sexual intimacy, the next night together would be in Vancouver, B.C. On that night, I was back to being his brunette alibi. But first, an unfortunate girl was chosen.]

Gary Ridgway was brought out of solitary confinement at the Walla Walla State Prison. The authorities wanted to question him about my first book. Ridgway remembered Daniel's favorite corpse. This was a young woman who looked like me, with long brown hair. The three men would visit the graveyard as a group to rape the girls, leaving behind their incriminating DNA with postmortem bruising, as forensic evidence of criminals and crime.

After I threatened to break Daniel's nose, he returned to necrophilia, or possibly he never left it. The look-alike corpse was a passive version of me. And his view transferred. The corpse was his wife. I became a walking version of the corpse, something that frightened him. I don't know where he found the young woman with long brown hair. But I know he brought her to the McDonalds restaurant in Kent, Washington, and bought her dinner. The McDonalds manager never forgot her and always looked for her again.

After the divorce, the counselors at Domestic Abuse Women's Network told me to do the things I'd been restricted from doing. I went to the McDonalds in Kent. A normal thing most Americans do. I was allowed to dine in. That felt accepting. I ate in quiet appreciation of my new freedom.

The Kent McDonalds manager came up to me and said, "I know this may seem like a weird question. But are you the girl who was with the man at the Ronald McDonald playhouse?"

"When they cleared the kids out of the playground?" I asked.

"Yes." The Kent McDonalds manager was relieved. "I finally found you. It has been eighteen months, but I never forgot you."

Had it only been eighteen months? It seemed much longer. Aloud I asked, "Did he hurt the children?" I had to evaluate whether or not to have children with him and that experience weighed in.

"No, we just had to clear them out," the Kent McDonalds manager explained.

"His parents told me never to take him to McDonalds," I responded. Then I added quietly, with irritation, "even though it was him taking me."

"He acts like he is receiving instructions," the Kent McDonalds manager gave the reason for our ejection from the restaurant.

"We separated," I informed him, so he won't worry.

"I just wanted to let you know," the Kent McDonalds manager said gently. As I got up to leave the restaurant and drop my litter in the garbage, the assistant manager whispered something in the manager's ear.

The Kent McDonalds manager asked me, "Was it this McDonalds?"

"No, it was the McDonalds in Auburn," I turned to answer. But that wasn't the answer he was expecting. His facial expression was blank at first, stunned, and then he returned to a look of worry. I turned to go out the door.

"Well, at least one of them came back," he said softly.

[Reflection: The McDonalds restaurant manager was referring to an incident in Kent. I was referring to an incident in Auburn. These were two different incidents where Daniel acted as if he was receiving instructions from the Killer Clown. The young woman in Kent was the unfortunate girl whose corpse was repeatedly raped. Ridgway's statement to the authorities confirmed my suspicion.]

When I spoke to the Kent McDonalds manager, I referred to my first date with Daniel.

The pastor told Daniel, "The secret to a great relationship is to treat even the cheapest restaurant as an expensive night out. That way, regardless of your finances, you can always have an expensive night out together, even if it is just McDonalds." The pastor smiled broadly. It was about perspective.

Daniel asked me if he could take me out for dinner. We drove to the McDonalds parking lot in his father's light green car. "My parents had to look hard to find a car with an interior that matches the exterior. Isn't that nice?" Even the steering wheel cover was wrapped in light green leather.

I nodded.

[Reflection: At that time, I didn't note the color. The outrageous splashes of seafoam green. I thought his parents' goal was to have an interior that matched the exterior of the car. I'm not skilled at identifying car make and model. To me, any car that is long in the front is a Buick. On further inspection, the car was a Toledo. A Buick doesn't come in a light green color.]

Daniel told me what he wanted and handed me a $10 bill. "Maybe we'll see Patches the Clown," he laughed. He disappeared to the back of

McDonalds. Completely disappeared. I went into the restaurant lobby and waited in line, assuming he would join me soon.

[Reflection: Patches the Clown was the character that John Gacy played at children's parties. John Gacy was the Killer Clown.]

As I was in line to order, a man with straight brown hair came running to the front lobby. The top part of his hair that he brushes over his bald spot is sticking up at an angle. He told the cashier, "Hey, we had to clear the children out of the playground." He looked over at me with an intense frown.

I was patiently waiting for my turn to order.

He asked the people in line, "Are you together?"

I put in the order, and I'm given the burgers in two "to-go" bags.

[Reflection: I was ordering too much food for one petite person. Two burgers, two drinks, and large fries clued him in I purchased for myself and another person who was missing from the line.]

I looked down at the "to-go" bags. "I was hoping for dine-in," I explained to the cashier. How were we to treat this as an expensive restaurant with to-go bags?

The cashier shook his head. "No dine-in," he asserted and moved his hand flat in a firm horizontal motion.

I didn't see Daniel. I didn't see him anywhere. I took the "to-go" bags and walked out into the parking lot. I looked for his parent's car.

Daniel was sitting in the driver's seat.

I went in and sat next to him.

"Patches was there," he said miserably.

I looked behind me at the playground and didn't see anyone. Most of the playground was out of view from the car. Maybe if I go out to look around the corner….

In the parking lot, I heard, "Hey, she just got in the car with him."

The Auburn McDonalds manager said, "I figured he was here with someone."

I silently wondered who they were talking about. I looked and didn't see anyone in the parking lot. I saw no one in the parked cars. I saw no moving cars. Maybe they are on the other side that is blocked from view, another part of the parking lot. There doesn't appear to be a road there. Maybe there is no parking lot either. I decided to come back another day to see what was on the other side of the restaurant.

Later I tried to find the McDonalds restaurant again to see what was on the other side of the parking lot. I was riding my red, extra-lightweight Schwinn bicycle. But I had a hard time finding anyone who would give me directions. It is hard to wander aimlessly on a bicycle in city traffic, trying to find a landmark.

"You want to know where the McDonalds is," the man on the street asked, "Why don't you just eat here?" He pointed to the left. I managed to find my way to Skippers. That was as far as I had gotten.

"I'm trying to see what is on the other side of McDonalds," I explained.

"You want to go to McDonalds to see what is on the other side," he reiterated. This was clearly unexpected. He looked up in surprise and paused. "Well, I've never heard of that one before."

I explained the incident during my first date with Daniel and how I searched the parking lot to see who the staff were talking about.

He soon identified the problem, "If there was no one else in the parking lot," he said, "They must have been talking out you."

This was a frightening realization. The McDonalds staff ejected me from the restaurant because Daniel had done something at the playhouse. Questions swam through my head. What in his upbringing would cause this? Would it be his mother or his father? Could I have children with this man? Did I want children?

Before the divorce there was counseling. The young adult pastor met with Daniel and coached him toward better hygiene. He wanted to see Daniel shower each day and brush his teeth twice a day. It was a basic request.

Daniel pushed back, "I don't see the purpose of taking a shower unless I have something to wash off."

Stirred Light Green

For my 21st birthday, I wanted to go dancing again. Daniel took me to a piano bar instead. We sat next to the piano, while the pianist played jazz music. I ordered an Angel's Milk, which had half-n-half and some sort of hard alcohol, possibly bourbon. This was his attempt at doing something special, but it wasn't something that interested me. I'm not fond of jazz music on the piano. This was boring, and I wanted to be alive.

We passed by a nightclub. People dancing could be seen from the highway. I pointed at them. It wasn't too late in the evening to join them. He looked forward in disappointment. He couldn't go in there, all the arms moving around.

At church on Sunday, the choir was leading the congregation singing, "He came from heaven to earth …"

"Do you ever feel like they are singing to you?" Daniel asked. I turned to look at him and he had a beaming smile watching the choir.

Daniel had a different taste in music. He was a fan of Larry Norman. And he liked a song about doppelgangers. He said he believed he had a doppelganger on an identical planet in the universe; and that he felt he received power from it.

"I think he is receiving power from you," a woman at the church said.

This was an interesting idea, but the bottom line is that I didn't believe in doppelgangers. The whole idea was rubbish.

Daniel stayed with friends on most nights. He came home one Thursday wanting me to try drugs. This was another turning point. I watched him pass out on the sofa. Then I looked up the drugs in my pharmaceutical book. I made a closer inspection of the label on the container and read that it was someone else's heart medication. A cardiac patient sold his medication for cash.

The event with the light purple blueberry pancake batter was the first turning point. It was clear that I wasn't going to be a pastor's wife. This situation with light green pills and light green fluid was the second turning point. I was the wife of a drug addict. It was a flaw that I defined my stature based on his occupation or habit.

Despite all of the violence, I tried to make the marriage work. But this was something I couldn't accept. From there on out, I sought a divorce. I slipped out of the apartment to gain advice from a friend who successfully divorced her husband. She was also in a position of being the financial supporter in the relationship, so we had that in common.

When I came back, Daniel was starting to regain consciousness. When he prodded me as to whether I tried the drugs, I lied by nodding my head. I didn't want to receive a beating for not going along with it. It is hard to make a marriage work when the value system and ethics don't match. The book, *"The Intimate Enemy,"* suggests that the more conservative partner partake in alcohol or drugs to create a balance in the relationship. I refused to stoop to that level. And I had lost my motivation to succeed in this marriage.

Filling in the Dark Space

I was in counseling at the Domestic Abuse Women's Network (DAWN) and learning how to navigate the legal system. My husband called me about a trip to the Vancouver BC Expo. I asked, "Will Ross and Bonnie come with us?"

"No just the two of us," Daniel replied.

"Should I put in a reservation for one bed or two?" I asked.

"Just one bed," Daniel replied.

Things were looking up. I was giving the marriage one last chance. Maybe, just maybe we could reconcile the marriage, or maybe this was the honeymoon period the Domestic Abuse Women's Network warned me about. The counselor advised, "Don't tell him that it's his last chance."

"Be sure to take out enough money for the trip," Daniel added.

Daniel expected me to pay. But one night together in a Queen bed might be worth the expense. Although, I was starting to wonder if he was the prostitute, and I was the John. I contemplated this while riding home on the city bus from Seattle to Kent.

"You're thinking of it wrong," a man on the city bus said with a smile. "A male prostitute is called a gigolo, and he has male clients, not female clients. Many male clients." He turned away and looked out the bus window.

Daniel and I arrived at the hotel and checked into the room. I went to bed with my keys in hand. I didn't want my car to be stolen again.

Daniel didn't come to bed. He left the room.

I was disappointed that he left, but at the same time, I was thankful he was away and not beating me. So much for our reconciliation or compensation for paying for the room. I peeked out the hotel room window and saw about five young men standing around my car. They moved away and my car remained in its parking space through the night.

When Daniel came back in the early morning, the smell was heavy and foul. I did not know what the smell was at the time. I now know it to be the odor of early-stage human body decomposition. It was the scent of death. I can't count the number of times I've smelled that smell. In the moment, I told myself the foul smell had to be something else.

Daniel walked straight into the bathroom and turned on the shower. When he came out of the bathroom, he said, "I left a towel for you."

I stood up and started to walk towards the bathroom. I wondered if the towel would be a hand towel.

"Don't turn on the light," Daniel instructed. "I don't want you to wake up the neighbors." He turned on a small reading lamp next to the bed for me to use the indirect light.

I rolled my eyes. There was no possibility that the people next door would be able to see a light on in our bathroom. There was a wall between the hotel rooms. I looked at the far wall above the toilet. It was solid. I could see the white paint. I imagined it was thick and fully insulated.

Then my gaze slid down the wall to the bathroom floor. Next to the toilet, there were three bath towels wadded up on the floor in a pile. On the bath towels, there was a yellowish tinge visible in the dim light. It was similar to a stain that is left over after trying to remove blood from cotton clothing. I looked up at the towel rack. There was one bath towel left. I glanced at the sink. He used three of the four bath towels and one fresh hand towel.

I didn't argue. I stepped into the dark shower and turned on the water. I had mastered a speed shower. I learned to take a shower quickly to avoid being pulled out in mid-shower, soaped up, and shivering cold before being allowed to finish the shower and rinse off the soap. Daniel's attempt at domination and control. My father said this gains respect, but respect wasn't the right word. Realization that I'm living with an unstable person was the message, along with fear. This morning, Daniel let me complete my shower without interruption. I dried off with the bath towel and then dried off my car keys, which I guarded at every turn.

"Aren't you tired?" I asked Daniel. He had been out all night.

"No, I slept in the backseat of a car," Daniel answered.

Whose car? I wondered. I hadn't taken my car keys out of my sight, not even to shower. I thought about setting them down on top of the back of the toilet, but brought them into the shower with me instead and then dried the keys off with my towel. I slept with the keys in my hand and the key chain attached to my left wrist above my watch. It wasn't my car he slept in. Is this what he does now? I wondered. Sleep in other people's cars. How can he feel rested?

Daniel turned on a brighter light now. We packed up our things into our overnight bags. On the way out, he told the hotel receptionist, "Sorry about the mess in the bathroom. My wife is on her period."

I wasn't on my period. Rather than argue, I simply said, "The bathroom smelled better after I took a shower."

Daniel quickly turned his head to give me a sneer. It was this look that concerned the hotel receptionist. The receptionist looked down and then turned to dash upstairs.

At the Vancouver, British Columbia EXPO we saw a 3-D display of Canadian geese. We had to stand in a long line. They gave us 3-D glasses at the door. We were told to keep our hands in our laps and not touch the seats.

It looked like the geese were flying right next to our faces. As if you could reach out and touch them. You could hear and feel the flapping of their wings. Our seats moved in response to the combined force of the geese, first slowly and then in a swift wide turn as they flew past. It was a 4-D experience! Hands down, it was my favorite exhibit.

We were tired of standing in long lines and came to an exhibit on Saskatchewan. This was a simple display of the Canadian moose. The hosts closed the doors and explained that they usually exhibit a providence close by and Alberta Canada was an obvious choice with the Calgary Stampede rodeo tourist attraction. But in all good conscience, they couldn't display that this year, due to the overwhelming problem of girls being kidnapped in northern Alberta. They asked us for our help if we knew anything about this problem.

Daniel said that he didn't hear them say anything about Alberta. He shook his head and had a blank expression on his face. This was odd. He was standing right there next to me.

[Reflection: The IRS was the first to identify a problem in that region. Money shuffled across the Canadian-U.S. border, along with packages of white powder. But human trafficking held a longer prison sentence.

My first thought was <u>not</u> Daniel. Although, I had reason to suspect him. If I examined it and counted correctly, he tried to human traffic me three times, not twice. The third time was best offer or free to the closest pimp, who would have nothing to do with a reluctant worker.

The Green River Kills at this time weren't a coincidence. Daniel made sure trafficked prostitutes didn't run into each other on the Sea Tac strip. He couldn't be found out to be a pretend brother of so many girls who had been sold.]

We found a German restaurant at the Expo. I left to use the restroom but kept my eyes on him. As I came to a place where I needed to turn out of sight, I mentioned to another customer, "If I take my eyes off him, something happens to the soup." Poison Control insisted that I do this as a precaution.

"What?" the customer asked.

"Food poisoning," I said.

"I'll keep an eye on him," he agreed and nodded.

"I'll be quick," I promised.

When I came back, the customer informed me, "He stayed put."

I walked back to our table with confidence. There wasn't another incident of Daniel slipping into the kitchen to poison the food. He allowed me to complete my shower without pulling me out in mid-soap. He let me sleep through the night without picking me up and slamming my body down onto the floor. And he didn't beat me. Overall, events were going okay.

I brought money. But I hadn't brought enough money for his alcohol. He insisted on buying beer at the German restaurant. He said he wanted each of us to have one. I hate beer. He forced me to drink some of his beer. I pushed my lips into a tight thin line and put the glass to my lips. The beer foam covered my upper lip. "There," he praised. "That is how I know you've had a good drink when there is foam on your lip."

When he turned the other way, I wiped the beer off with a napkin. He hadn't noticed. None of the beer had gotten into my mouth.

He told me to drive in the left lane to use less gas. He physically beat me while I was driving home on I-5 through downtown Seattle, unlatched my seat belt, and periodically pressed his foot down hard over mine on the gas to make the car accelerate and go out of control. In one swift move from unlatching the seat belt, he was grabbing the steering wheel and turning it hard toward the center divider on the freeway. Cars came alongside honking. He was trying to kill me.

I mouthed the words, "Help me!" to the passing cars.

Daniel turned to look at the other drivers watching us and watching my face. "What is it about you that people take one look at your face?" He moved off of me enough for me to steer the car towards the right-hand lane.

"Drive in the left lane!" he yelled. He looked to his right and jumped in his seat. We were on a double overpass. It was a long way down.

"No, I'm driving in the right lane and going slow," I assert.

"Slow down," Daniel said quietly. He looked around him. "The other cars are keeping pace with you." The cars were creating a protective buffer on all available sides of my vehicle. "Okay, drive the speed limit." He backed off and stayed in his own seat the rest of the way back.

At DAWN I learned, "A situation looks different from the inside than it does from the outside. That is why it is hard for others to imagine our situation."

"What did you do at EXPO?" my mother asked me after the trip.

I told my mother about the 3-D display of Canadian geese.

After I obtained a protection order, Daniel went to visit my parents. When my mother asked Daniel what he enjoyed most at EXPO, he didn't immediately respond. She told him what I said as my favorite exhibit, and he shook his head.

"He waited to hear her answer to the question. He already had in mind to refute it and say that it didn't happen," one of the male guests noted.

My father responded with a, "Hmm," that was almost a groan.

Daniel told my mother, "We didn't see that exhibit, because Karen was too frightened of it."

Later my mother confronted me about the difference in our answers. She said, "It doesn't matter," and gave a sideways smile.

She said this because she started to believe Daniel when he contradicted me. She believed that I was crazy. Daniel couldn't torment me in the bedroom anymore, so he tormented me through my parents.

Later I ran into a man who went to EXPO, and he attended that same exhibit. It was exactly how I remembered. I'm very thankful for moments like these that restore my sanity

Lying Dog

When we divorced, I informed the staff at the church. The Sunday School Director had a relieved smile and said, "You're better off." She remembered Daniel's lesson on doppelgangers.

"We divorced," I told the other young marrieds. "I got a protection order." I was advised to let people know.

Karen One's husband nodded, "Did he try to strangle you?" He remembered the time I asked him who had purple-toned skin. I forgot the conversation.

"He tried to crash my car into the center divider on the freeway," I answered.

He was surprised. "I believe you," he replied. "That's not the direction I thought things would go."

When he said this, I was thinking about the direction of the car, going off the road towards the center divider. I didn't remember his thought that I would die of suffocation. I turned to walk away.

"I've been praying," he said.

I didn't believe in prayer then, but it was working.

"Opposites attract," another man at church said, "because they have similarities." He looked at me and added, "Usually God has me say that to someone who is divorced."

"I am divorced," I admitted with a heavy sigh.

The man quickly turned to look at someone behind him, and then he turned to look at me.

"I don't have anything in common with him," I said, sadly. "Camping was supposed to be our common interest. He wanted to break camp at the crack of dawn," I looked down and mumbled with a frown, "with people after us." The memory wasn't clear. What was happening at those times?

"You mean, like, with scent dogs coming after you?" he asked.

"Not exactly, that," I paused. I couldn't remember any dogs. The sound of a bear came to mind. Wasn't that a bear? It wasn't the sound of a dog. Why weren't there any dogs? I wondered. "That might have helped. I could believe a dog." I clarified, "I mean I could believe a dog is telling the truth." I wasn't making sense.

"You are tired of lying dogs," he said. He related my comment to infidelity. "But you aren't him," he said with certainty.

I asked the pastor, "Why did he think I was talking about infidelity?"

"Because that is the reason most people get divorced," the pastor answered. I found out later Daniel told him I was unfaithful. And the pastor believed it.

Hardness of Hearts

Most people understood, except for my family. "Jesus doesn't believe in divorce," was their comment.

My mother had me recite the verse about Jesus saying Moses only allowed divorce because of our hardness of hearts.

"Were you unfaithful?" they asked. A couple isn't allowed a divorce unless the woman in unfaithful. The woman isn't allowed to leave a violent marriage unless she cheats on her husband. This can't be the correct way to interpret the verse.

Daniel asked my parents not to tell anyone that we were married, "I don't want to be implicated."

"It's probably because he wants to become a minister," I said. The annulment through the church gave both of us a chance to start over. New beginnings. I smiled with contentment. We were both moving forward in our own direction.

"I don't think that is it." my father said with a frown.

[Reflection: Daniel was using the situation to encourage people to determine that I was mentally unstable, was potentially dangerous, made false complaints, and imagined that I was in marriages that never took place. His stated intent was to have me found mentally incompetent; after doing so, he planned to become power of attorney over my finances.]

Cutting In

I married Bill in July 1993 in Yakima County, Washington. I bought a two-bedroom house. Six months after we married, I noticed a knife was missing from the knife block. The knife had a weathered wooden handle.

"Where did you get it?" Bill asked. "I'm trying to figure out what happened to it."

I hesitated to answer. "How was I found so quickly?" was the question running through my head. That doesn't seem possible. And I didn't know who "who" referred to. I wasn't sure who the knife came from. I found it outside my bedroom window in downtown Yakima. I realized someone might have intended to use the knife to gain access. I sharpen my own knives, so I added to the knife block.

Bill found broken glass around the house. "I think someone else is getting into the house," he said.

"Victor?" I asked. Victor was a friend of Bill's who came by the house, even though he had a warrant for domestic violence. This was a situation I was not happy about.

"No, it wouldn't be Victor," Bill answered. "I need to leave." He had started a job as a security guard.

Bill told me that someone was getting into the house, and then he left me alone. I sat down on the floor in the hallway and hugged my knees. I wished he understood how terrified I was. Maybe he would have stayed home to comfort me. But I understood that he should go to work. I listened to the silence after Bill reversed the car out of the driveway.

Karen Roberts

I heard two soft footsteps on gravel. Rudy, our neighbor, would have stepped with three heavy footsteps. It wasn't Rudy. Then there was a noise I hadn't heard before. I turned my head. I thought about getting up to run and see who it was. But I froze. I was too scared. The next day I inspected the driveway. The noise seemed to have come from near the front of the garage. I never opened the garage door. I stood and stared at the garage and then went back into the house.

Later I bought a sheet of thick plastic to replace the broken window in the spare bedroom. I was sent to buy a sheet of glass but came home with plastic instead. The salesperson insisted that I buy the plastic. Bill went into the garage to grab caulk and a caulking gun. When he came back into the house, he said, "I don't remember the garage door opening that smoothly before." He wondered if I had oiled the garage door.

I told him, "I've never opened the garage door." He didn't think I had.

A $100 bill was missing. My mother had suggested that I keep extra money in a book, and then she called back later to ask which book I put the money in. It didn't make sense to suspect my mother. She lived too far away. It made more sense to suspect Bill. He had access to the house. The situation created accusations.

The gravel in my driveway was slowly disappearing.

Death of the Killer Clown - May 10, 1994

On May 10, 1994, John Gacy received a lethal injection. During the stay of execution, Daniel reassured himself that the authorities didn't really want to serve the death penalty. They would rather delay. Now this thought was shattered. Daniel worried lethal injection would happen to him, so he called my father.

My father said to me, "I had to work hard to calm him down and reassure him that he didn't need to worry." He spent hours with Daniel on the phone. My father thought it had something to do with my recent marriage. My father asked, "Did you do something to upset him?"

"No," I said with a frown. I wondered why Daniel contacted my father at all and how long this had been going on. My father didn't seem to refer to Daniel as a distant memory, and there was a tone of fondness in his voice. I had a protection order. There shouldn't have been any contact at all. And why was Daniel worried about lethal injection. "Which states offer lethal injection?" I asked. I wanted to figure out why he called.

My father thought I was heartless and said, "You're missing the point."

[Recently the investigator said, "I wish your father hadn't reassured Daniel, because lethal injection is where things are heading."]

Camping Gear

It was with Bill that I had my children. I'll skip the details, because it isn't important for this story. Bill and I separated in 1999.

I had a yard sale, which was a moving sale. Rudy, our neighbor, came over and swung open the garage door. There was a ladder upright in the middle of the garage. "Did someone use this for a loft?" Rudy asked, pointing to the boards overhead.

I took a close look at the boards. "Is there room for a loft up there?" I asked. I knew a person didn't need much space if all they intended to do was sleep.

"Heat rises. Maybe they used it for storage," Rudy decided. That is when Rudy looked in the corner of the garage and found the folded army cot. He knew what that was and how to assemble it. He set it out for the yard sale, and it was a quick buy. I grabbed the sleeping bag, which looked familiar, and added it to the camping gear.

I assumed it was Bill's sleeping bag. "What do you want me to do with your sleeping bag?" I asked him over the phone.

"I don't have a sleeping bag," Bill answered. He never went camping. I kicked myself. I had gotten things confused. I must have bought an extra sleeping bag and forgotten about it.

I moved everything that didn't sell with me to graduate school. The camping gear went into my storage space at the college.

At the graduate school in Pullman, I had a block on my account, along with the protection order. This prevented any domestic problems at the school.

My father came to visit and asked my roommate to ask me for the locker combination for the storage. I refused to provide it. They didn't need to ask for my combination in front of guests.

I told my parents that I found a café that serves a Manhattan. This was my favorite sandwich; a tuna melt with bacon and tomato. Grilled cheese sandwiches combine with tuna and a BLT. Crispy outside crust with a gooey cheesy middle and soft tuna center supported by fresh tomato slices and the smoked flavor of bacon. Served with a glass of lemonade.

[Reflection: I wasn't eating kosher foods at the time.]

Daniel convinced my parents that a Manhattan was an alcoholic drink. And he claimed I was an alcoholic boozing it up at college.

[Reflection: The block against domestic abuse isn't offered at their satellite campuses, which became a problem later. Daniel's portrayal of alcoholism extended to the satellite campus, and contributed to my expulsion. Daniel's false information was added to an anonymous third-party complaint alleging that I was stalking my professor and masturbating outside his office window.]

I moved back into my house in Yakima after two years of graduate physics and a year of bioengineering. I accepted an Electrical Engineer position at Conley Engineering, programming water treatment and wastewater treatment plants. Daniel must have been stalking me. When I joined a soccer team, one of my teammates contacted my work and claimed that I didn't have a physics degree.

She worked for the city police. "How can I be wrong?" she asked another soccer teammate.

"How can you be right?" he answered, "You've never talked with her."

"I talked with her," Jeff said. He was one of the drafters at my work. He knew my soccer teammate. "She is very sorry about what she said."

There were comments from my work supervisors that could only be from someone spying on me. I was asked to sing a song from *"The Little Mermaid,"* to show evidence that I was childish. "Sorry" doesn't pay the bill or clean up the false information. I took a different technical job across the state.

Moving On

I sold the house, moved, and bought a new home. I intentionally didn't tell my parents. I learned not to trust them. My parents poured money on Daniel to encourage him to get back together with me. They gave him money each month and put him through college for a degree in psychology. In this way, Daniel and my parents blended as one. The protection order violation blurred across through third-party harassment, like a sandstorm on an ocean beachfront, wide, expansive, and uncertain where one ends and the other begins.

Someone called my parents and asked them about my purchase of a house. My parents did not confirm my real estate purchase. The caller assumed I was lying about buying a home. The caller also asked my mother if I earned a bachelor's degree. My mother remembered going to a ceremony, which she thought was my college graduation, but she wasn't sure. She remembered sitting in the bleachers at a football field for something and watching people walk past. The questions were confusing. The caller expected my mother to say, "No."

The state was confused about how I could buy a house without informing my parents. For these reasons, the caller assumed I had lied to my employer. The caller informed my employment manager of assumed fraudulent activity. That is, misinformed my coworkers that I purchased a home to convince them to help with the move. And providing false information about my college degree. Just to clarify, again, my information was not false.

Karen Roberts

I was terminated from my employment and not given clear information as to why, so I had no opportunity to defend myself against the false accusations. I could have easily addressed the issue with documentation, real estate records, and contracts, as well as diploma and official college transcripts. If they had talked with me instead of with my mother, these misunderstandings could have been avoided.

"You're looking at this case wrong if you think she needed to inform her parents before buying a home," the state was criticized later.

My parents learned that I had in fact bought a house and they drove Daniel out to show him where I lived. They knew I had a protection order, but they didn't take it seriously. "This is what you will be getting if you get back together," my parents prodded with big smiles of encouragement. So, in addition to losing my electrical engineering job and having a new mortgage payment, I now had a stalker. My parents did not warn me that they informed Daniel where I lived. If I was only renting, I would have been able to relocate to a place where he wouldn't be able to find me.

Stalker Returns

I sometimes took the bus to save on gas. But on those days, my gas tank went down more instead of less. I was trying to save a few pennies. And this wasn't working. I used less gas when I drove the car every day! And the oil was dirty. I'm normally green footprint conscious, but I had to shift away from that.

The driveway was freshly re-graveled in October 2016, but the gravel was gradually disappearing again. I started to see this as normal.

It was not long before things started showing up at the house. One item was a fist-sized rip on the window screen of the dining room and a brownish-red smudge of thick fluid on the window glass. The substance was too transparent to be paint. It was thick like mucous. It appeared to be blood, too large for an insect or spider, and closer to the size of the smear of an adult thumbprint.

My daughter GJ said, "It was bright red at first," when the smudge appeared on the window.

At my work, I was asked to sing "*I Love the Way You Lie.*" This is a song about learned helplessness in an abusive relationship. I was asked questions about things in my house that only someone who was in it would know. I didn't have visitors. This was further evidence of a stalker. One day at work, a coworker received a telephone call to ask me, "Why are you wearing a hair clip, instead of a barrette?" and then to report the answer back to the caller. Two others received requests to look over my shoulder when I typed my password and report back the answer. Another received a call to encourage me to stay at an expensive hotel and charge the bill to my employer. I refused to do this, but I was reprimanded by my supervisor anyway as if I had. It is very difficult to keep employment while these pranks are taking place.

The New Nature Trail

I went to visit my parents' farm. We took a walk through the forest, old trees planted before my grandfather bought the property. It was a leisurely stroll. My father always loved the way God created the lovely shades of green. The moss hanging from the trees looked like the hair of an old gypsy woman with an inviting story to tell. The sword ferns, male with their white spots and female with their yellow spots, sprang out of the forest floor. Wide, dark green maple leaves danced overhead. The pine needles provided rich soil for a unique ecosystem of insects. Fuzzy black and orange striped rollie bugs crawled across the path and provided a strong contrast to the variety of greens. It was similar to taking a walk through a fairyland. You almost expected a tiny mythical creature to fly past and then land on your nose. It was a beautiful wetland.

A friend of theirs, who they didn't name, had encouraged them to forge a trail through the forest for nature walks, fresh air, and exercise. The path was made by a small tractor. It was just less than six feet wide and wound through the trees, over towards the road and then angling back along the edge of the cow pasture. With each turn, the only view was more trees, showing off the forest. It was secluded and peaceful, walking through something larger than yourself and older than your ancestors.

The tree roots were exposed and intersected across the nature trail. The roots looked like netting pulled tight in one direction. It provided the right amount of traction for the uphill walk. In some places, the green moss covered the tree roots and yellow moss tinged the edges. The effect looked like delicate green lace had been woven onto the path. I was hesitant to step onto the beautiful wonder.

We came to a pile of fresh dirt in the path. We all looked down and veered to the left side of the trail. "Occasionally something is helping us with the trail," my mother laughed.

A molehill would have been round and about one foot across. This dirt mound was rectangular, instead of circular. It was too wide to have been made by a large animal. The dark brown fresh dirt was about three feet across. "How many?" I asked nervously.

"Just a couple," she answered with nonchalance.

My father turned his head to the left to look behind him and face my mother. He had an intent look, and he said, "I think it is just one." He didn't want to argue.

I looked over the landscape. There were no other places of fresh dirt. An animal that burrows would have made more than one entrance. This wasn't done by an animal. This dig looked man-made.

As my mother passed, she turned her head back to look at the fresh dirt. She had an uncomfortable look on her face. Then she looked down at the packed dirt on the rest of the path made by the tractor as she continued to walk back to the house. "I prefer the path from the tractor," she decided.

May 25, 2020

George Perry Floyd Jr., who was born on October 14, 1973, in Fayetteville, North Carolina, and raised in Houston, Texas, worked as a truck driver and security guard in the greater Minneapolis, Minnesota area. As a bouncer at a nightclub, his backup was police officer Derek Chauvin. Each week for more than a year, the nightclub had employee meetings, and George Floyd and Derek Chauvin attended. When the COVID pandemic hit, George lost both jobs. Meanwhile, Derek remained in his position as a police officer.

In Minneapolis, counterfeit bills started to surface. On May 25, 2020, a Cup Foods grocery store clerk reported that a black man paid with a counterfeit twenty-dollar bill. Derek Chauvin was one of four police officers who arrived on the scene. If we were in an alternate universe, it was fortunate when Derek saw and recognized his co-worker George. Derek, knowing George's character, then realized that George didn't know that the twenty dollar bill was counterfeit, so he asked George if he could give him a ride home to have a talk. Derek knew this approach would have George aid in the origin of the counterfeit twenty. It was fortunate to work together with George again, this time to get to the bottom of the counterfeit bill production.

Unfortunately, we don't live in that universe. On television, watchers saw George Floyd die while pressed under Derek Chauvin's knee. Unfortunately, we need to examine the errors in our society to learn how we ended up with such a dramatic difference in the outcome. Despite George's distinct physical characteristics, Derek didn't recognize him. Even after more than 50 employee meetings, which they both attended, Derek didn't take a good look at George. Derek had two reasons to dismiss George Floyd. George was black and he was a security guard instead of a "real" cop, a rent-a-cop.

Derek Chauvin saw George Floyd sitting in a car with two other passengers. The police officers forcibly removed Floyd from the car and handcuffed him. George didn't know what he had done. A white police officer was restraining him. All parts of his body went into a panic. "What did I do? What did I do?" George cried. He didn't know the twenty-dollar bill he used at the grocery store was counterfeit.

On the flip side, Derek Chauvin had a police report to respond to. He found the suspect and started the pursuit. To Derek Chauvin, he was restraining any other suspect on the street who was resisting arrest. This suspect was large, black, and athletic. The suspect is harder to restrain, yet more susceptible to death because of fentanyl and methamphetamine drug use. Derek restrained George Floyd by kneeling on his back and neck for nine minutes and 29 seconds. Two other police officers also restrained George. George's dying words were, "I can't breathe."

All of the muscles in George Floyd's body relaxed and went limp. He became motionless. Without his heart beating and without his blood distributing heat, his body was cooling to the temperature of his surroundings. Due to gravity, his blood shifted towards the street, and the color of his skin turned pale. Derek Chauvin continued to restrain George for an additional two minutes. The medical examiner found that George Floyd's heart stopped while he was being restrained and that his death was a homicide. A second autopsy showed George Floyd did not have a previous medical condition that attributed to his death. Derek Chauvin was found guilty of second-degree murder and treating George "with particular cruelty."

In Portland, people began to congregate to express their objections to the treatment of George Floyd. They rallied with George Floyd's last words, "I can't breathe." They congregated for months, living in tents as homeless people, pulling down statues, drawing graffiti on buildings, breaking windows, and destroying beautiful artwork.

Employees at local stores were drawn to the protests at the Multnomah County Justice Center in Portland, Oregon in 2020. For months, the protests had become their entire world. One local employee said, "I did feel a deep sense of guilt if something was happening, and I wasn't out on the street as well."

Some protestors were abducted by a group of men dressed in camouflage. They were driving an unmarked civilian black van as they grabbed people up. It was assumed these were federal enforcers, a part of Trump's America. But it was later proven that the team was rogue. The black van was not government issue.

"It was distressing," a man on the street complained. "You would be walking alongside someone and talking with them one second, and they would be grabbed and thrown into a black van the next."

One of the peacekeepers said, "They know now that these are not federal agents. The local police are looking for the offenders and taking the matter seriously."

The protests increased momentum. A Wall of Moms appeared on July 18, 2020, in downtown Portland at the Multnomah County Justice Center, chanting the words of George Floyd before his murder, over and over again, night after night. These were mainly white suburban women who sought a display of solidarity. This was followed by a smaller Wall of Dads a few days later and a Wall of Veterans who joined on July 24.

The moms wore yellow. The group of dads wore orange. The veterans wore white. The legal observers from the ACLU wore bright blue. The National Lawyers Guild wore green. While black was the default color of protest.

Some locals stayed away from the protests for a few days. But they came back out in time to see the protests at their height. The downtown park blocks were packed with new protestors.

A rabbi complained, "It's so wearing."

"Why don't you take the night off?" one of his congregants asked.

"I don't want to go," the rabbi confessed, "But I feel like I have to go. I need to be a positive influence. They need to see me there."

I interjected into their conversation, "So much of my life I've felt that way. I wish there was a way I could take a night off. Sometimes I just need to let go."

The rabbi asserted, "No, I need to go. I'm worried about what will happen if I'm not there. People see me and they believe peace is possible. It sets a different tone."

As much as I tell myself to let go, my situation seems unending. I'm fighting something larger than myself. I can't defeat it. I can't take a break as easily as just not going downtown. It is unseen evil, and it springs up again out of nowhere.

In Portland there were riots. Two rocks were carved into the size and shape of softballs. One rock was thrown at the left temple of a police officer and hit him in the helmet. Then another rock was thrown at the left temple of a police officer and hit him in the helmet. Neither of the police officers died, but each was taken to the hospital with a concussion. This was an intentional hit, not a miss.

This action was similar to Daniel striking me on the head with a wooden spoon and the bowl taking most of the impact, the way he did when I made blueberry pancakes. He knew that even with the protection of a helmet, there would be injury, but not murder.

Tempered Glass - Downtown Seattle 1985

I remember when the Columbia Building was constructed in downtown Seattle. The 76-story high-rise building, the tallest building in Washington state, was constructed with tinted tempered glass. At the time of its construction, the 933-foot building was the tallest on the West Coast. The construction began in 1982 and was completed in 1985.

On an early Monday morning, the glass installers approached the frame of the Columbia Building. They packed in their lunch boxes, and put on their hard hats and steel-toed boots. This was the final touch on the outside of the building. The construction workers explained the building is designed to withstand the forces of the winds from Puget Sound. But the glass is vulnerable to a single-point force. They had to be careful while handling the glass. The point force destroys the glass to be installed, but it will not shatter the glass.

Daniel listened to the construction workers in fascination. He was out all Sunday night, visiting the homeless in downtown Seattle, and had parked in the garage across the street.

Riot Broke Out - Downtown Portland 2020

The tide from the protests could not be held back any longer. A single rock was thrown through the bank window, tempered glass designed to withstand blunt force, but susceptible to a point force. The rock made a single hole in the center of the window, but the rest of the window remained intact.

The police heard and saw the rock speed through the bank window glass. A security alarm sounded. The police assumed that they were the targets. The police were there to protect the people assembling, but they fled. The riot had begun.

The people in the crowd scattered. The rabbi heard a man ran from the riot screaming, "There's blood splattered on me, and I don't even know whose it is!" Everyone went into a panic.

Nothing was stolen from the bank. Later the police wondered what the intent was.

Another Nature Walk

I took another slow walk through the forest with my parents. They hadn't gone on a nature walk for a while. I looked around. This wasn't the lush green forest that I remembered. The dirt was wet in most places, creating mud, matted mud, drips of mud on the broad, dark green maples leaves, dark brown mud, brown mud, light brown mud, tan colored mud, wet mud, runny mud, drippy mud, and splashes of mud. It looked as if the dirt was scattered and rained on by differing amounts. Some mud patches in the rain longer. Soil in different stages of rain exposure. There was fresh dark brown dirt in other places. The dirt was scattered without thought to the beauty of the green forest. The trail was forged to admire the natural, God-created beauty of the wet land forest.

I asked, "When you cleared the path, what did you do with the debris?" There was no answer. I repeated the question.

My father looked around at the landscape. All debris was cleared out long ago when the trail was forged. He came to a sudden stop. "Hey, we didn't do this," was his only response.

"Maybe the neighbors?" I asked.

"The neighbors didn't do this," my father determined.

"Why am I sinking?" my mother asked, looking down at the soft mud below her. The spot in the path was becoming lower under her weight.

"What are those piles of dirt?" my father asked. "He told us he didn't want us to go for a walk. He said he was concerned about us tripping and wanted to ensure our safety." He was thinking out loud. "Why did he encourage us to forge the trail for exercise and then tell us not to use it?" He turned to face my mother, "Why did he tell us to leave the shovel out?" he asked.

I didn't dare ask who "he" referred to. That would create a complete clamming up and no answers to obvious questions. Instead, I asked, "Outside? The shovel was left outside?" I knew better than to ask who. This isn't because I knew who. I had no idea who. "Who" was a troubling unanswered question. It was only because the conversation would completely stop, and all answers would cease if I asked the question of "who." I asked, "Would you do this with a," I paused, "shovel?" It seemed like too much mud, too many dirt piles.

My mother responded, "You wouldn't do this with a shovel." She was beginning to sound distressed. She was standing in the path in a place where the dirt was smooth. "Why am I sinking?" she asked.

My father turned around and extended his hand to pull her out of her spot. The mud was now indented there, in a well larger than her feet. The smooth path had a visible ridge and firmer soil to the north. The tree roots that interlaced across the forest floor, were severed and missing. There was no strategic traction for the uphill climb, which was now much steeper. Erosion? Too quick for erosion.

My mother accepted the lift to more solid ground. "That isn't the point," she said with some irritation. "Why was there digging in the path?" she asked.

"Or at all," I asked. The green forest floor was spattered with ugly tosses of brown. Sword ferns were bent under the weight of the dirt.

There was a bend in the trail. The area behind the bend was hit the worst. This was where the path was closest to the road. "Maybe he came in with a truck," my father decided. He had an idea of who did this, but he wouldn't say who. "Let's go back," he said. We walked back to the house at a brisk intentional pace. The conversation had ended.

A family left a note on the front door of my parents' house saying they were interested in buying the property. The property was not listed for sale. My father called them. They told my father they were interested in keeping the property as it is and not developing it. My father loved God's handiwork in the trees. He expected the old growth forest would remain. He agreed to sell.

The buyer approached my mother with the completed paperwork for the sale and said, "Your husband wants you to sign this." My mother was not consulted for the sale, even though it was her property. My mother was gifted property by her parents in exchange for care in their old age. She was to safeguard the acreage for the family. She included my father on the deed, which wasn't what her parents had wanted. My mother wanted to protect the property if she were to die. This was property she cherished. Nonetheless she signed the paperwork.

The new neighbors rented a large backhoe. They used their backhoe to remove the forest my father loved. They got rid of the timber. They cut down all the trees, pulled up the roots, and burnt the remains. They leveled the land to create "possibilities". But the tree roots weren't the only thing they dug up. The new neighbor's backhoe pulled up a dead body. In the act of pulling up the roots, they dug up a skeleton.

My father admitted that Daniel was at his house. Daniel was the one who suggested making the trail for nature walks and exercise. Daniel told my father to leave the shovel out, and then told them not to use the trail for fear of tripping.

"What time did he leave?" I asked.

"8:00 pm. I know for sure, because I was wondering why he was waiting so long to go," my father replied. My father was Daniel's new brunette alibi.

"Did he say where he was going?" I asked.

"No, he didn't," my father answered. "Dan arrived at the house; and he had a weird smile on his face."

I know that smile. It was the Killer Clown smile.

"I put my complete trust in him," my father said. It wasn't a confession. He didn't see the problem.

"He used the shower," my mother said and gave a shrug.

The smaller bathroom with a shower was off of the garage. There were no black spots on the ceiling, but my mother is an exceptional housekeeper.

Dan discussed what was happening in downtown Portland. "He asked us how we felt about the protests," my mother said. "I don't know why they decided to pick Portland to congregate. The moms came to show solidarity. There are plenty that never returned home."

Sub USB

A man approached me at work, "What is the most valuable item you have in your house?" he asked.

"A USB," I answered. "Even if it is just recipes," I shrugged.

"I just realized ..." he paused, "I'm not going to tell him."

"Oh, he's right outside," a woman said, she turned to leave "I'll tell him."

"Wait," the man grabbed her, "There's something wrong with you if you think you should tell him. We need to have a talk."

But another woman overheard the conversation, and went outside to talk to the man waiting.

Later at home, my daughter GJ received a telephone call. The man on the phone wanted to make sure I was screaming in anger. But the wrong USB was destroyed. GJ said it was my father on the phone. But the FBI had told me that Daniel was making calls and pretending to be my father. So, I don't know which one it was.

Despite the effort to derail my witness statement, I was able to write it on paper and turn it in at the right time. I passed by a tabloid stand with the title, "*Serial Killers and the Women Who Love Them*". I was thankful I wasn't one of those women, only to realize I was. But that puts me back to defining myself based on what he is doing. That is no different from expecting to be a pastor's wife and then wanting out of the marriage because I'm the wife of a drug user. Who I am isn't defined by what Daniel is or what he is doing.

A song lyric comes to mind, "You told me who I am. I am Yours." I am a child of God. God defines me, not my ex-husband's occupation.

I sat down on the black leather chair, underneath the picture of the cross. "He's in prison now," I told a woman at the church at the Ladies Bible study. This was a moment of relief.

She was sitting on the black leather sofa. She gasped in realization. It was good that she followed the information so well. She immediately identified a problem.

"You're right," I said. "He's in prison, but this keeps coming. Someone else is doing it."

She nodded.

My daughter moved out. Lydia, the Siamese cat she adopted, died and I was entrusted to conduct the burial. I buried the cat under the cherry tree. That was in 2021, before Daniel was taken into custody.

After Daniel went to prison, my mother confessed that he spoke to her, "He saw you burying Lydia and decided it was a good place to bury things."

I hadn't thought about the cherry tree. There is a sink hole on the east side. I continued to chant to my mother, "I got a protection order." Daniel wouldn't know where I live if they hadn't driven him in their car and pointed the house out to him.

A local police officer wrote in the file, "She doesn't even know what type of trees are in her yard."

"I know all the trees in my yard, the species, where they came from, whether they were transplants or from a seed," I argued. "A cherry tree was planted from seed in the location where an oak tree once stood. The cherry tree and the oak tree roots created a hybrid. It volunteered to grow next to the pie cherry tree and the Rainer."

The man reading the log entry looked up at me and said, "He was thinking that it's an elm tree."

"It produces cherries," I countered, shaking my head.

"Okay," he said with a smile, "It's an elm tree that produces cherries."

My cherry tree in bloom

When I was in jail for filing a false complaint, that wasn't false, my parents refused to bail me out of jail. I hadn't lied. The university assumed I was too young to have been married. They didn't check my date of birth, because that could be age discrimination. The FBI verified that I hadn't made a false complaint. The investigator talked with the school and reported, "The school said they are dreadfully sorry."

Now contrast that with my father insisting on bailing Daniel out of prison. Daniel was on trial for murders that he actually committed. My father would bail out Daniel, but not his own innocent daughter!

Who keeps the harassment coming? My father was the one who convinced Daniel to yank me out of the shower in mid-soap. The shots in my bedroom, when I was seventeen, were done just after I qualified to train for my black belt in martial arts. Initiating violence would disqualify me from the training. It was another way of not letting me finish what I set out to do. Another way to exert control.

At my daughter's church, a woman asked if her, "Is your father in prison?"

My daughter was volunteering at the church and busy setting up the room. She was irritated at the interruption and the woman's question and answered, "No!" Her father isn't in prison. He isn't supposed to be. As far as I know, my daughters never met my first ex-husband. Even though he broke into the house, raided our food, and caused a variety of problems. Usually, he remained unseen. And we blamed each other for the various messes and packrats around the house.

The woman interpreted my daughter's answer to mean that I was wrong about my first ex-husband being in prison. But she had miscounted my ex-husbands. She thought my first ex-husband was my daughter's father. Before this misunderstanding could be corrected, she was off telling the church staff that I was mentally ill.

Diary Entries

I've been harassed five times in four weeks. These are marked on my calendar.

August 21, at a small business meeting, a woman told me my business isn't legitimate. She noticed my empty glass on the table in front of me and accused, "You've been drinking!"

I responded, "I grabbed the thing that had the least alcohol."

One of the business owners noticed and went to talk with her. She was not a business owner, and the event was exclusively for local small business owners.

August 23, 2024, A rogue MSW is trying to suppress my testimony, although it is needed by the FBI. She is removing my books from local bookstores, under the claim of "customer confidence."

August 28, 2024, at an adult education event, a woman asked a man to ask my supervisor to ask me about an invention that I designed. The man came by to argue with me, while a woman was standing by listening in. She didn't understand the physics or math, but she was evaluating my mental health, not understanding the education and honors that I have. The doctorate in science at table next to me, who is also in aerospace, agreed with my math. Did the woman watching notice that I had agreement from a PhD in science who specializes in aerospace?

September 6, at a coffee shop, a woman from Washington was accessing the Oregon file through a back door access. The Oregon file isn't locked and allows entries. The Washington file is locked. The woman refused to identify herself or her business when asked.

"I know how to use the database," she said.

"Apparently not," I responded.

"I can add to this file. I think it is the Oregon one," she said. "Here is the warning about being prosecuted in Washington and Oregon, all the way back here. Look at all the entries since then."

The entry on April 11, 2024, is located too many entries back to notice. It reads, "Using this file will result in prosecution in both Washington and Oregon."

"Most of the entries are by one person," she noticed. "They wanted someone else to write her book. That is why they gave it to someone else, not because the information was wrong." She thought it was for consumer confidence. "She is from out of the area. Oh, those poopheads. No wonder the Attorney General's Office is trying to shut them down."

I know who must have made those entries in the log, the man who got me terminated from Amazon. I can only take so much emotionally, so I left.

September 13, 2024, at the coffee shop, another business owner said about the woman who was there the week before, "I thought she knew something." He had believed her.

October 1, 2024, at a financial seminar, a woman asked me if I was drinking. I had an empty soda pop can in front of me and bottled water. No wine. No alcohol.

The person next to her said, "Look in front of her. She wants to bring Muscato, which is the wine with the lowest alcohol."

It produces clarity for me to realize that the only reason they refer to me as a drunk, is because they think a tuna sandwich with bacon is hard alcohol. The real sin is the bacon.

November 28, 2024, I told my immediate family about my first ex-husband's murder convictions. They were surprised, because they were told my report was false.

November 30, 2024, my extended family was misinformed that I was in legal trouble. The investigator went down the same rabbit hole of contacting the mother, instead of the murder witness, and doing interviews over the phone instead of in person for a murder case.

Previously, at my choice, the FBI had promised me royalties for the books I wrote and published instead of a cash reward for assisting in Daniel Bondehagen's capture in Troutdale, Oregon and for providing details that linked the murders to him, to which he later freely confessed. The authorities had praised my accomplishment.

But now the authorities silence my achievement and suppress my account. And the investigator had not read my books. The publisher of my first book told me this was illegal. This is taking place without court action, so I have nowhere to appeal.

My mother confessed that she was pressured to tell people where I worked, which made it impossible to maintain employment, even after Daniel's capture. I was portrayed as turning a man in who was confused as to why he would be charged, instead of helping with the capture of the most dangerous man in world history.

My mother contacted an authority for the arrest record of Daniel James Bondehagen and received an immediate response. This number was shown to some members of the family. They had to absorb the financial impact first. They had invested money in him, and it was clear this would not produce a return. The nature trail was recalled as an after-thought.

December 5, 2024, a social worker who was in training at providing training to a college intern showed up at my workplace. They had received false information about me from a textbook that was published by a university. The seasoned social worker told him, "There is no authoritative body. You didn't check." In this case, there was no court action to support the contact. "This isn't the sort of thing someone would choose to investigate," he said.

"I was told this would be a good case to do when I was being trained," the trainer said to his supervisor.

The seasoned social worker was disappointed that trainers weren't checking and how many other social workers were not trained to verify.

For social workers, this case is the one they remember most, because it is the first one they learn about. However, the information in the textbook is false, which is what makes the case interesting.

Conclusion

There are residual problems. I see the failures. But I don't see what God sees. God is the author of my story. God sees the wins. I wish I could have skipped being a doormat. But God saw Daniel hit me while I silently prayed. And God formed a plan.

There is no statute of limitations on murder. And Daniel's victims will receive their voice, from the camper at Sol Duc Falls, to the victims in Vancouver, British Columbia, Canada, the camper in northern Washington state, the camper northeast of Seattle, those in Banning, California, the homeless, the protestors, and all of the other tent sleepers that I missed. God can use all things, even bad things, at the right time. And there will be consequences. Because our God sees.

When I wrote my first book, I started the story from the time I heard about the Green River Killer's first murder and information Daniel wasn't aware that I knew. If I started in any other place, I wouldn't be alive right now. And I started at the right time, when Daniel was stalking me; and he had all points bulletins out for murder. This was God's timing. God protected me. And God used it, because God can use anything.

A red and white vertically striped flag, with a large red maple leaf in the center, flew outside in the wintry wind. The building was plain and constructed of cement. The rooms inside were ordinary and pale gray. There were no windows. No toilet, only a pot. Residual smells from the pot lingered heavy in the stale air.

"When will I move to my permanent quarters?" Daniel asked the prison guard. Daniel glanced behind him at the room, turned around to face the guard, and then smiled tensely in emphasis. He assumed the stay in the holding cell was an oversight. His question was met with silence.

"May I have a pencil and paper?" Daniel asked.

Daniel thankfully accepted the pencil and passively scribbled a poem onto the paper. The authorities were nearly done for the day. Daniel took the pencil and held it firmly in his right fist.

Daniel knew the difference between a vein and an artery. "Do they teach you that in class?" he asked me when I studied Human Anatomy & Physiology in our apartment in North Queen Anne. "Piercing one vessel instead of the other creates a faster bleed." It was one of those interruptions I chose to ignore.

Daniel purchased #2 pencils in bulk. After I started a new family, there were several packages of pencils that appeared at my house. I was tired of finding pencils that weren't sharpened. So, I diligently sharpened all the pencils and placed them in a wooden container. It was unnerving to find more unsharpened pencils, and to watch them roll onto the floor as we walked past the bookshelf.

I found unsharpened pencils along with many other odd things; a brown sleeping bag, a California king sized seafoam green satin comforter, a green and gold plaid blanket, an army cot, a red overnight bag, a red jacket, men's long underwear, a blue bath towel, and two life vests. The unexplained items caused me to become fearful. I was regarded as "hypersensitive to stalking." This reaction furthered Daniel's efforts to make me appear too incompetent to manage my own finances, creating a foot hold for his con.

A pencil was the only weapon Daniel needed. He had practiced skill, and he didn't miss. He quickly spun around with a force and speed they couldn't stop. He stood up tall with his feet together.

"Whoa!" the prison guard gasped. The prison guards reached out to stop Daniel's right arm. But it was too late.

Bright red blood seeped around the shaft of the pencil and poured down the left side of his neck. The pencil was used to write this final note, "Killing was the only thing that made me feel alive, and it killed me not to commit murder."

This morning, I read these passages in Romans, "A married woman, for instance, is bound to her husband by law, as long as he lives, but when her husband dies all her legal obligation to him as a husband is ended. ... In the same way you, my brothers, through the body of Christ have become dead to the Law and so you are able to belong to someone else, that is, to him who was raised from the dead to make us live fruitfully for God." Romans 7: 2, 4

Being free is a relief, but it brings uncertainty. However, I know God has a fruitful life ahead of me.

www.ingramcontent.com/pod-product-compliance
Lightning Source LLC
Chambersburg PA
CBHW060948050426
42337CB00052B/1718